The Mysteries Of Excellence

The Mysteries Of Excellence

Graduating from Challenges to a Champion's Arena

Emmanuel Goshen

Published by Edson Consultancy

© Copyright Edson Consultancy 2016

THE MYSTERIES OF EXCELLENCE

All rights reserved.

The right of Emmanuel Goshen to be identified as the author of this work has been asserted in accordance with the Copyright, Designs and Patents Act 1988.

No part of this publication may be reproduced, stored in a retrieval sytem, or transmitted, in any form or by any means, electronic, mechanical, photocopying, recording or otherwise, nor translated into a machine language, without the written permission of the publisher.

Condition of sale

This book is sold subject to the condition that it shall not, by way of trade or otherwise, be lent, re-sold, hired out or otherwise circulated in any form of binding or cover other than that in which it is published and without a similar condition including this condition being imposed on the subsequent purchaser.

ISBN 978-0-9930661-9-1

Printed and bound in the United Kingdom

CONTENTS

DEDICATION i
APPRECIATION ii
PREFACE v
INTRODUCTION 1
WHAT IS EXCELLENCE? 6
FACTS ABOUT EXCELLENCE 12
KNOWING YOUR PASSION 21
UNDERSTANDING YOUR PASSION 34
LEARNING FROM THE BEST 45
GATHERING THE REQUIRED INTELLIGENCE 57
EMBRACING PROFESSIONALISM 63
MANAGING RESOURCES EFFECTIVELY 74
BEING PROGRESSIVE-MINDED 82
STRIVING FOR PEAK RESULTS 90
CREATING A LASTING AND POSITIVE IMPACT .. 96
TAKE THIS HOME 104

OTHER BOOKS BY EMMANUEL GOSHEN

1. The leader's supplement: A major platform for high performance leadership
2. The 7 Laws of Productivity: Make Your Vision a Reality
3. The 7 Principles of Transformation: Accomplishing your goals with the right insight
4. The Mysteries of Excellence: Graduating from Challenges to a Champion Arena

DEDICATION

The success of this book is dedicated to the Almighty God, the foundation and pillar of wisdom and understanding. It was He who inspired me to write this book.

APPRECIATION

Except the Lord builds the house, they labour in vain that build it: except the Lord keep the city, the watchman waketh but in vain (Psalm 127:1) (KJV). Dedicating this book to the Almighty is not enough, I must first be appreciative of Him for through Him and by Him I become whatever I am today, it is all by His grace that I am able to attain the milestone.

I also appreciate various supports I received from my immediate family, my loving and beloved wife Rachel and lovely son Edward; to my caring sister Beatrice and friends for their huge sacrifice in allowing me to write and publish this book. To my mother, Pastor Mrs. Victoria Majekodunmi, and father, Engineer James Majekodunmi I say thank you for your inspirational words in bringing me up. I appreciate Prophet Adefenwa and his family, my sister Janet and her wonderful family. My thanks also go to my uncle Mr. Solomon Majekodunmi, and Prophet Moses Olurin and his family for their support and prayers. To Prophet Larry Osoffo, Pastor Eric Duru, Pastor Eric Amankwah, Apostle Sheriff Jacobs and Rev. Mother Oguntoye, I appreciate your immeasurable love and support.

To a lovely father in Christ, Evangelist Moses Kolawole Solaru who stood beside me and instilled the required wisdom to help me through rough times and become the man I am today, the unbeatable fact of history would foster reality and you can never be forgotten in my mind. Never would I walk pass through this side without appreciating another father, brother and friend Evangelist Paul Babatunde Soile and his wonderful family for their passionate love and support in which mere words can't describe. My thanks likewise go to Dr. David Soile, Pastor Joshua Bandele, Prophet Barek, Dr. Tayo Ogunmefun, and Evangelist Richard Dele Moronfolu for their outstanding love and words of encouragement. I cannot forget to be grateful to my class teacher and Brother Mr. Sunday Banjo and his family. I say thank you to Evangelist Abraham O Ayoade for his professional advice.

The following people at one time or the other have touched my life and I must be very thankful to them; they include Dr. Oluwasegun King and his family, Madam Grace Ogolo, Evangelist John Maforinkan, Dr. Deborah Titilayo Nunayon, Pastor and Mrs. Adeyemo, Mr. and Mrs. Okondu, Mr. and Mrs. A.A. Ademola, Prophet Elijah Alabede, Mr. and Mrs. Owamoboye, Mr. and Mrs. Ejimagwa, Mr. and Mrs. Adekoya, Mr. and Mrs. Akinbobola, Mr. and Mrs. Omogbai, Mr. and Mrs. Williams, Madam Sheri Adekomolafe Edu, Mr. and Mrs. Aghaghon, Mr. and Mrs. Obembe. Dr. Martin Ehigianusoe will always be remembered in my prayers for the amount of time and effort he invested in making this book a reality.

I feel humbled and respectful in appreciating Venerable Superior Evangelist Olusegun Olarinde, Mr. and Mrs. Obafaiye, Mr. and Mrs. Akinola, Mr. and Mrs. Ajibade, Mrs. Janet Sims, Mrs. Sarah Francis, Mrs. Alayo, Pastor Akin Soyoye, Mr. Abayomi Domingo, Mr. Vicent Eni, Ms. Toyin Abraham and Madam Fatima Tiamiyu Abioye, Pastor Yinka Ogunlola and his family, Pastor Paul Oyelade, Pastor Debo Adegoke, Pastor Isaac Omotayo, Pastor Philip Abiola, Pastor John Adeyinka, Pastor Segun Stephens and Pastor Mrs.

Funmi Fadairo, Ms. Busayo Asade, Mr. and Mrs. Afolayan, Mr. and Mrs. Kuku for your love and contributions in making this book a reality. Mrs. Philippa Gittens and her lovely family are worth to me more than any kind of treasures and have a special place in my little heart for their encouragement, which enabled me to go miles further than I thought possible.

Looking back on my years in public service, I would remain grateful to all my wonderful colleagues starting from Mr. David Green for his outstanding support throughout my time with him, Mr. David Taylor, Mr. Osagie Ezekiel, Loveday Cole, Mr. Ogho Tunkia, Mr. Mich Boreman, and Elder Peter Nwachukwu for their friendly and brotherly relationship all my years of service making it worthwhile. You will all be remembered in my prayers. At this point, I am glad and proud to say that you are all wonderful and worth more than what mere words can describe. I would like to appreciate the wonderful effort of my editor and proofreader in persons of Chrissia Tyles and Brunella Costagliola.

PREFACE

The richest man who ever lived, King Solomon, wrote in his book of proverbs, *"Seest thou a man diligent in his business? He shall stand before kings; he shall not stand before mean men"*. (*Proverbs* 22:29). Considering this fact mirrored his personality, experience, and achievements, King Solomon was known for his unique wisdom and wealth. In fact, it was recorded that he had many horses, a lot of gold and other valuable items. He was the wisest man who ever lived and wrote the three most inspirational books in the Old Testament of the bible. By taking an inside look at the Biblical verse, *"Seest thou a man diligent"* (i.e. mindful, careful and persistent), it is easy to notice a continuous effort towards accomplishing something unique or of a certain significance in a consistent and focused manner. For example, the expression *"In his business"* can refer to work, purpose, goals, dreams, or even visions. However, '*business*' could be regarded as a legal or an acceptable activity in achieving one's ambition in both life and career. The word *"works"* requires a deep level of commitment to distinguish it from other contenders on the same field. However, it is not a matter of being competitive but rather taking on the challenge of performing at the peak of one's ability, regardless of what the situation might be. Aiming higher and striving towards rendering a quality service is the best way to become extraordinary. In taking a critical view of the words *would stand,* it can be noticed that according to King Solomon, this simply means such a person would be separated from the crowd and his spectators because their efforts have created a unique place for them. This being so since their efforts have reflected a specific achievement that has spoken louder of them than any trumpet or anyone else would have done. The words *before kings* simply means that the achievers would always be recognized for their remarkable efforts towards a *particular* achievement and remain significant history makers and directing the positive impact created for younger generations to follow. The word *kings* could be referred to those who determine and make events happen, be it a change or a transformation. In England, the British monarchy is well known for awarding knighthoods to those who are being recognised for significant contributions to the national life and other good causes, whose influence has made a positive impact in the lives of the citizens, ranging from actors to scientists, politicians, schoolhead teachers, musicians, authors, novelists, and industrialists. This type of recognition is usually based on meritorious service and it is meant for those who are able to attain landmarks in their area of specialty without excuses. Recognition needs to be deserved or else it might lead to public outrage. Considering the last part of the statement, *he shall not stand before mean men;* achievers would dwell in the midst of other achievers and not just anywhere. Mean men, according to the passage, refers to those who are aware of the changes that occur as a result of someone's positive impact on others. Yet they do nothing to contribute, but criticize every good effort of those making good things happen simply because they are being regarded as stakeholders. Diligent men are often seen as role models and could mentor many to excel in their lifetime and referred to as legends afterward. In a nutshell, the journey to excellence would always begin with a diligent attitude regardless of a man's talents, skills, background, privilege, and determination.

The book of Proverbs 18:16, says a man's gift makes room for him and brings him before other great men. A diligent man is well known for showing intelligence in his works which serve as a guide for them to remain on the right track and become outstanding in their various fields. With all things being equal, a diligent man is bound to excel at the fullness of time. Analysing King Solomon's accomplishments even further, he built the first temple that is of great significance in history and also became one of the wonders of the ancient world. King Solomon's ability to be and remain diligent made him wiser and gave him the required skills to become an excellent diplomat, trader, and collector as well as a patron of arts and inspiration to others. His unique wisdom became a huge source of wealth and riches for him which was as a result of continuous learning. His ability to attain excellence made him a respectable figure in the presence of other dignitaries and royalty. In reading through the Book of Proverbs, I discovered the only way to avoid living a hard life at an old age is by working hard and intelligently at one's youthful stage. Sitting on the fence without doing anything reasonable is the road map to nowhere.

The need for excellence has always been attached to daily life; being happier is one major product of attaining greater heights because more things become easier. As written in the seven principles of transformation, the process of transformation begins with an attitude of having a positive and strategic mindset. Likewise, attaining excellence is always a result of having extraordinary thinking and a positive imagination. However, imagination needs to be relevant to the desired future.

While attending a seminar a few years ago, I heard an introductory speaker make a call for the exchange of the twenty-pound note he was holding for ten pounds. The audience was watching. Some took it as a joke, a trap or a game, while others doubted if he knew what he was doing. Some kept on thinking that it could not be true, while others considered it as an opportunity but were afraid or confused to take action. Then, while some never knew what to do, a young man jumped forward and grabbed the twenty-pound note and gave the introductory speaker the ten pounds he was holding. At that point, everyone shouted because they had realized it was a golden opportunity they all had missed out on because the event cost ten pounds and the young man received ten pounds cash profit because of his approach towards that opportunity. The main speaker mounted the platform and started his presentation by telling the audience that our approach towards information and opportunities determines what we achieve and attain in life. It is reasonable for us to never allow opportunities to pass us by and no matter how small an opportunity might be, getting and taking action would always have a cost attached to it. Yet, the end result would always be of an expected and significant value, which could make a huge impact in our lives. Mighty buildings begin with the act of a pen being lifted to design it. As a coach, I got to discover that a person's mentality is the most common stumbling block from attaining excellence. Some of the audience were considering the cost of grabbing that golden opportunity which might be a risk in a certain way but yet when the young and diligent man grabbed it, every other person in that room wished they had grabbed it. The event cost ten pounds in which the young man received ten pounds profit because of his ability to take required and reasonable action at the right time. Diligent people aiming at excellence would consider that cost as a major issue because they did not get up and take action. Rather, they considered the value and quality of every single situation they faced before taking the appropriate action which is the soul of excellence. Bear in mind, having a positive mentality fires up the ability to act in you towards achieving results and later differentiates you, while a negative one only beautifies your excesses by making them reasonable and make you remain the among the crowd, which I refer to as stagnant mentality. The second stumbling block is associating with the class of negative people, those who see the little shining light in you and give a kindling advice rather than fuelling it. Those who would make you believe you cannot make it; opportunities and greatness are meant for those from privileged backgrounds. The fact that people would only give what they have and tell you what they know doesn't mean it is reasonable to settle for less, apart from the education received outwards, a reasonable person still needs to educate himself because external advice could lift or ground you.

Attaining excellence is never by magic but as a result of diligence in one's reasoning and action. A friend of mine once told me, money can't buy you happiness. I replied, "But money can buy those things that could make you happy". Business and life are similar to the moving train that never waits for anyone. Those who know what to do but refrain from taking action at the right time due to fear or anxiety would eventually suffer a painful loss because they are good at being ignorant. Associating with the class of negative people is as helpful as handing yourself to a destiny and dream destroyer. Those who would fill your mind with negative facts, distractions, and irrelevant issues also make them look relevant to be considered and invested upon. The bottom line is these negative people would never be any help or provide a solution when things go unexpectedly. Attaining excellence is about performing an extraordinary and desired service for the purpose of humanity which requires having the right skills to exhibit at the right time.

Muhammad Ali, for example, was considered the greatest heavyweight boxer in the history of the sport and he was also recognized as the sports figure of the century. He once said: *He who is not courageous enough to take risks will accomplish nothing in life.* I am sure this was his major belief which empowered him to attain heights in the boxing world. His excellence in his boxing career wasn't just a matter of skills or talent but his mentality during his prime made him become what he was. Taking a deep insight from his quote, it is clear that he had gotten a transformed and strategic mindset towards what he was doing and where he was aiming to be. His belief regarding what it is required to excel inspired his daughter Laila Amaria Ali to go miles in the boxing world, resulting in being named as the Super Middleweight Champion by the International Boxing Association in 2002 and Super Middleweight Champion by the International Women's Boxing Federation in 2005. In other words, his impact was able to motivate his daughter to excel. Another one of his powerful quotes was: *"I hated every minute of training, but I said, 'Don't quit. Suffer now and live the rest of your life as a champion'."* It is now clear that attaining excellence in any career takes struggle and pain, but the ability to endure and preserve would always position anyone for better opportunities which could tailor one towards greatness. Another inspiration from that quote is that Muhammad Ali was consistent in working towards becoming a world boxing champion which helped him walkawayfrom working hard at his old age. However, consistency enabled him with resistance to those things or situations that would have stopped or drawn him backward. The Seven Laws of Productivity book also explains in detail the impact and importance of being consistent. In relationship with his quote, I would like to take an insight from the book of Galatians 6:9, *"and let us not be weary in well doing: for in due season we shall reap, if we faint not."* The reality behind this verse is the need to maintain consistency in all endeavors. I remember watching a motorbike race many years ago on television when one of the participants started his journey with high speed and carried on with the same speed while spectators were hailing him as the potential champion. With a short distance to complete the race, he made a sharp bend and fell off the motorbike. It took him a few minutes to get back on track, but two of those behind him maintaining a reasonable speed had overtaken him and he ended up in the third position. While the champion of the day was granted an interview, I expected it to happen because he had maintained a reasonable speed and was careful at every bending point in a consistent manner before arriving at the final destination. My point is, overdoing things at times can result in disappointment if proper care is not taken. This book will be considering and analyzing THE MYSTERIES OF EXCELLENCE in an in-depth view and with a practical approach to capturing the message of the preacher.

INTRODUCTION

Bill Gates was once asked during an interview session if he had to start all over, how he would go about it? He replied, *"As a networker."* One thing was clear from his reply, the world has gone past the industrial age and is now in the information age, also known as the digital age, and that was the major reason he was able to go miles by making the digital age a necessity for both business and other aspects of life. The world is now being operated as a global village. Obtaining business contacts, booking medical or any form of appointment is now being done digitally. In recent times, online learning and education have become the best alternative for students due to its convenience, mostly the ones with special needs. In reality, the world would carry on expecting great ideas from great achievers; those who have gotten solutions to long-lasting problems and faced down challenges for the benefit of mankind. Having a great idea doesn't make you recognized until the idea is being put to use and producing unique outcomes. This accomplishment requires having an empowered mind and not a lazy one. Barack Obama once said, *"If you're walking down the right path and you're willing to keep walking, eventually you'll make progress."* In summary, the desire for excellence requires having the right direction and maintaining an accurate focus, commitment, and consistency. The result would eventually be worth telling and an accomplishment to

THE MYSTERIES OF EXCELLENCE

be proud of, providing the person desiring to excel is progressive minded, which will be later explained later in this book.

As wars are not fought and won by the field marshals alone, likewise, attaining excellence in life is never a one man game. Recording victory at war fronts would require service and commitment of a trained and equipped army of soldiers in which each soldier has a specified role to play. These roles would be attached with an expectation in terms of how strategic operations and executions are carried out at the war front. The point is that execution can never be possible without understanding and abiding by the principles of engagement that requires leaders, who are being faced by challenges of communicating, to connect with others in terms their committed service. In reality, without engaging others towards understanding and sharing your vision, you are embarking on the journey to nowhere. Dr. John Maxwell once said,

> "Leaders must be close enough to relate to others, but far enough ahead to motivate them." "Leaders must be close enough to relate to others"

Without the required relationship to get connected with other like-minded ones, it would be almost impossible to accomplish a goal. *But far enough ahead to motivate them* – means to make others think and see outside the box, and motivating others which as a result helps to beat their fears and carry on towards achieving the unexpected limits. King Solomon was able to build the historic temple that was the idea of his father with the support of others in which he leads, motivated and communicated with. Take it or leave it, without effective communication, it would have been difficult or impossible to lead and motivate others towards the historic

INTRODUCTION

achievement. However, in any organization where communication is not effective or considered with less importance, they're bound to confusion and commotion, not attaining a specific and reasonable direction.

Nelson Mandela will always remain a hero in Black history due to his impact in fighting for freedom for his people. He achieved international recognition for rebuilding his country which was once a segregated society. The fact remained he attained heights with other comrades who struggled through the aestheticism period for the sake of freedom and harmony. In the documents of his trial in 1964, he said:

"I have fought against white domination, and I have fought against black domination. I have cherished the ideal of a democratic and free society in which all persons live together in harmony and with equal opportunities. It is an ideal which I hope to live for and to achieve. But if need be, it is an ideal for which I am prepared to die."

It was clearer than ever that he was able to excel because of his strong determination that inspired himself and others to carry on the struggle and he ultimately paid the sacrifice that made him a legend.

In simpler terms, excellence is not about money overflowing in one's bank account or gaining unlimited political influence for personal advantage. Rather, it is about identifying and being sure of one's direction with a good understanding of what it requires to excel in that same direction and not struggling in another person's direction. I doubt if anyone could come in flying colors doing so because of the strength and expectation of a duck is different to that of an eagle. It's about walking the right part, having known and understanding one's calling and purpose that defines one's stand. It is also realizing the impact you have made among other standing heroes at a particular point in time. It requires self-discovery and seeking various ways of improvements that could be attained by studying the lifestyles of great leaders, in terms of their strength and how they utilize the best of every opportunity and information that comes their way.

Reading motivational books such as The Leaders Supplements, The Seven Laws of Productivity and The Seven Principles of Transformation, as well as listening to inspirational tapes or CDs from various authors and speakers does help, to a large extent, in terms of fostering more insights. Another important fact is the journey towards excellence starts small, in which anyone who wishes to excel needs to cherish. One must also keep track of their mistakes and successes to serve as a platform for equipping their mind in facing down greater challenges. In King David, the father, and predecessor of King Solomon was confident at defeating Goliath based on his experience with fighting against the lion and also a bear, which attempted to destroy a sheep from the flock he was entrusted to shepherding. The same legacy made him reach heights in his lifetime. Before becoming king, he endured a lot of unpleasant situations and never gave up in light of facing challenges. Attaining excellence is also about taking the right action at the right time. If David had missed fighting against the lion and the bear or hide from the situation by pretending to not see them, his mind wouldn't have been well-equipped in taking further responsibilities. He most likely wouldn't have gotten the courage and boldness to face down Goliath who had brought the nation of Israel to a standstill for forty days and nights. However, without defeating Goliath, he wouldn't have been celebrated by the people because his victory was reflected as someone who knew what to do and how to get it done. It was a major

INTRODUCTION

expectation from the people in his journey towards excellence, the situation made him threat to King Saul, his predecessor, which lead to the increase of his challenges. However, he never gave up in doing the right thing at the right time. His diligence in terms of *what to do* and *how to do it* enabled him to face the challenges of King Saul by staying away in exile, waiting for the right time to return to Israel and become the king who was said to be anointed by the Prophet Samuel. Another lesson from David's life makes it clear that the journey also required reasonable endurance, which enables us to live while keeping our hopes and aspirations alive in a positive manner, bear in mind never a testimony without a tale of testing one's faith of reality and value. Referring to Muhammad Ali's quote previously mentioned, *"I hated every minute of training, but I said, 'Don't quit. Suffer now and live the rest of your life as a champion"* – it is clear that he endured the pains of training for a greater significance. The gospel truth is, to excel in any endeavor, giving up is never and would never be the best alternative, as commonly said, he who runs from fighting would always live another day to fight. According to Marta, never give up, and be confident in what you do. There may be tough times but the difficulties you face will make you more determined to achieve your goals and win against all the odds. To achieve excellence, you need to prepare ahead for challenges in a strategic manner, to present your possible best and always seek for improvement measures in attaining the extraordinary.

WHAT IS EXCELLENCE?

"Perfection is not attainable, but if we chase perfection we can catch excellence."

-Vince Lombardi

One of the greatest teachers and philosophers in Chinese history, Confucius, once said, *"The will to win, the desire to succeed, the urge to reach your full potential... these are the keys that will unlock the door to personal excellence."* Taking a critical view at this quote, attaining excellence in our everyday life comes always as a result of our determination to succeed in any endeavor or profession we are passionate about, excellence is personal but requires the support of the right people and resources to attain. However, excellence always requires facing reality and making the right choices both in life and business. It requires knowing both your strengths and limitations in terms of exhibiting one's skills and reflecting core values. To hit it home, the fact remains unchangeable, excelling in any field first requires having the potential to go the extra mile and the capability to develop and improve beyond limitations. Excellence can be attained by focusing the expected energy on what is of greater value. Usain Bolt was able to go miles and make waves in the world of athletics because he discovered his strength and focused his energy on it. However, this fact reflects the impact of the

WHAT IS EXCELLENCE?

law of focus according to the seven laws of productivity. He began his career in a positive manner while in high school which attracted the media's attention. In the earlier stage of his career, he failed to qualify for the finals at the 2001 IAAF World Youth Championships in Debrecen, Hungary, where he made his first competition appearance. He never faltered or gave up as an option, leaving the world of athletics. He ventured into something else that he might end up being frustrated about due to lack of the required vision to excel in the alternative direction. It would be easy to get discouraged due to limited qualities or no strength to fuel the passion for him to go the extra mile in fulfilling his full potential in the alternative direction. Nonetheless, he was able to see and use his early failure as a platform to learn and improve through consistent practice. This was due to his urge to reach his full potential by creating the will to win and the avenue to unlock his personal excellence which brought him to the state of prominence. The word I say to myself is 'don't quit', just like Muhammad Ali, the legendary professional boxer, is reflected in the successful pattern of Usain Bolt. Likewise, the law of consistency is a third of productivity and it has enabled Bolt to stand before kings in the world of sports.

In order for excellence to be attained, it requires the attitude of striving. According to John W. Gardiner, *"Excellence is doing ordinary things extraordinarily well."* The word *extra* has separated the situation from a common state by injecting a change which requires marginal efforts to create the gap for others in similar situations. Searching for the definition of excellence, I could refer to it as a high mountain which requires those having a great passion for climbing and getting to the top.However, without having passion in any endeavor, it becomes so easy to lose focus and be distracted or discouraged and end up in a waste by seeing no meaning in one's efforts. Moreover, no matter what the case might be, excellence requires doing and focusing on one thing at a time to avoid conflict and confusion. In climbing the mountain of excellence, one needs to be determined by being ready to give more than is expected and should also bear in mind, the impact of one's action, mostly in the aspect of making a difference to the world around them. In my research, I discovered that getting to the mountain top starts by placing one's first foot into an available pot hole by the side of the mountain while holding to a strong role to serve as an aid. The higher you attain, the more the level of fear and doubt increases but the reality is, some would see the act of climbing as being risky and might consider giving up as the best option. Meanwhile, others would see it as challenging, enabling them to increase the level of their confidence and competence by focusing on what matters to them, which is arriving at the top of the mountain top within their expected timeframe.This requires the use of intelligence to know the right and next pot hole in which to place their foot and make further moves. Another discovery is that by arriving at the mountain top depends so much on one's ability to follow through and follow up. For example, climbing the same mountain that others have considered to be meaningless or boring, going the extra mile in finishing the task that could produce expected results and making a huge difference in one's life with glorious moments. Another important fact while climbing up is the ability to take extreme care of one's self because mountain climbing is not a matter of doing things or taking steps. Rather, it requires knowing what to do and when exercising great caution.

Moreover, attaining excellence is never a one of achievement, it's about having the continuous *'will to win'* as said by Confucius. It creates the avenue to discover more of one's ability in attaining more heights, mostly during prime days and it's paramount to learn from every experience,

WHAT IS EXCELLENCE?

record and gained what has been learned from others. Excellence is a drive from within and not from the outside. However, the desire to excel is exclusive to the fact that whether someone else appreciates it or not. Yet, some people always feel delighted and cherish the result of excellence that people achieve, mostly when the achievement is the first of its kind. Excellence is not about forcing one's self to please others. Rather, it is the ability to put in one's effort aiming at a peak performance in an effective manner that mirrors satisfaction and fulfillment in being the best they could be.

For better understanding, excellence is about solving problems and providing exceptional service to clients and other stakeholders within a reasonable timeframe while also sharing the industry's best practices with the aim of staying ahead of competitors. It's also about improving operational programs and processing an effective manner. From the gathering of successful people's lifestyles for excellence to be attained in leadership, it requires listening to and focusing on stakeholder's needs and remaining committed to their organization's overall success. Listening to and focusing on a stakeholder's need enables leaders to view these needs from a critical point of view before implementation, which is the secret of successful teamwork. Leaders need to be responsive while considering and sticking to the expected quality and service standards in meeting such needs. Another fact about attaining excellence is that it requires the ability to nurture relationships in an intelligent manner for the purpose of strategic alliance and benefits. This ability is a vital component in any negotiation environment because a well-protected brand and an excellence reputation would always command advantages at any negotiation table. It takes leaders to be creative in order to facilitate problem-solving ideas, challenge existing obstacles or barriers and break new grounds for the purpose of progress and prosperity. It also helps in finding innovative approaches toapplying existing concepts to complex situations.

According to Dr. John Maxwell, excellence is the gap between average and exceptional. It is the ability to exceed limitation and expectations and consistently deliver superior quality. In developing habits of excellence, there is a need to gain influence and stand out from the crowd. Cultivating a culture of excellence enables an organization to attract new customers including clients for businesses and winning their loyalty, which is a strategy to sustain them for as long as they can. Taking insight from the various definitions of excellence, I see this concept as an act of integrity matching one's behavior with positive values by being a person of his words. Integrity reflects honesty and diligence. Achievement is often recorded at various stages of a particular mission or project and could be temporal if not well maintained and sustained, mostly when aiming at a long-term vision. An achievement having a lasting and positive impact in a generation with the ability to sustain it makes it a legacy and also gives it the definition of excellence. In my findings of the definition of 'Excellence,' I came across various definitions. But, the most meaningful one to me is:

> Excellence is the product of a conscious effort of hard work, diligence, perseverance, and consistency to stand out on an act, which when seen can be respected, admired, and can be emulated by others.

In a nutshell, having a zealous mind towards one's real and right direction in a realistic manner is another platform in attaining excellence. Nothing else is worth celebrating more than an extraordinary performance being attained such as breaking the current champion records. Usain Bolt had become an icon in the world of sports due to his ability to

WHAT IS EXCELLENCE?

break the previous 100 meters world record with a time of 9.63 seconds. I am sure his performance is not the purpose of fashion or records alone but serves as a challenge to the younger generation of athletes.

From attaining to sustaining excellence requires having a great or strategic mindset. Before excelling in any direction, people with great minds never wait for what they would get or earn from carrying out a particular task. These people are always interested in making contributions towards making ordinary situations extraordinary which are a major step in creating a positive impact that enables them to live a meaningful and rewarding life. Great minds are those who face challenges with passion and assurance of light, being in-between and at the end tunnel and are never afraid of anything because they've been empowered byfaith and not fear. The unchangeable fact that faith and fear can never dwell on the same train, one needs to be eliminated from the other. People with great minds are positive influential figures because of their ability to see and view challenging situations in an innovative manner as an opportunity to test their strength, mostly intelligently, they think before they act or speak their mind. They believe in building better relationships and make lasting connections that require them to perform at their peak due to their realistic expectation of a brighter future that makes them and others successful in everything they do.

FACTS ABOUT EXCELLENCE

As King Solomon said in the book of Proverbs 4:7, *"Wisdom is the principal thing; therefore get wisdom: and with all thy getting get understanding."* Regardless of anyone's life ambition, the significance of both wisdom and understanding can't be underestimated. It takes wisdom to be a strong and courageous character in the midst of challenges and come out of with flying colors. However, wisdom provides the insight to see beyond others, mostly while in the shadows of the past. Many achieve a lot and attain heights during the early moments of their lives but decline due to their inability to maintain and sustain what they've achieved, which is a result of lack of wisdom. Wisdom is an inspirational gift and cannot be acquired in school like that of education, nor either does it comes with age. Likewise, wisdom is what it takes anyone to understand their actions and the reason for them along with the value attached to the mission embarked upon. To remain focused and determined towards attaining, maintaining and sustaining excellence, wisdom enables anyone to put the right knowledge to use at the right time and at the right place. Also, having the correct understanding of a strategic situation enables leaders to give the right direction.

Regardless of the current situation of anyone, acquiring wisdom and understanding could enable discovering the seed and part towards greatness. Those two are powerful parameters in illuminating ignorance and breaking above

FACTS ABOUT EXCELLENCE

limitations because they enable you to operate fearlessly. Wisdom facilitates the ability to focus and drive towards one's goal because it creates the platform for your passion and hope to remain alive while helping in building the required trust to carry others along. Wisdom enables you to build, maintain, and sustain your integrity in becoming a relevant and excellent person.

Attaining excellence is the foundation of the beginning of a legacy. It requires anyone to first believe in themselves in order to have the self-confidence to face down challenges and move further in one's calling. In fact, self-confidence gives marginal strength to be successful. To attain excellence, it is wise to learn from the best and find the reason why others failed. In most cases, lack of adequate preparation, passion, strength, resources, opportunities, and choices do affect excellence. As a business coach, I discovered that great achievers are those who have worked on their skills and habits which required to be excellent and successful. It is all about hard work and not games.

Attaining requires endurance but in a reasonable and realistic measure, excellence is in those who never give up in whatever they are passionate about because of their strong desire to succeed. Passion is what motivates us to take action, it deeply moves to see obstacles as challenges and not as a reason why we need to stop or give excuses. It serves as the fire within and compels anyone into motion. Passion gives us the ability to be touched, moved, and inspired. Passion is at the core of excellence that guides a vision from getting lost. Excellence is never a one-man game or band and not just surrounding oneself with people but the right people, who believe and trust in your vision or mission. Surround yourself with those of intellectual ability and the capacity to help attain and achieve one's dream.

It is about helping others in being the best they can be,

which is another platform for discovering one's strength and creating more opportunities for expanding one's wealth. Creating a culture of excellence is another way of attaining it because it is about having the required strategy and set of tools in place for getting things done. Creating a culture of excellence is about facing reality in what it takes to succeed and injecting a result-based ideology inthe focus of anyone wishing to attain heights in his field. According to Harry Paul, popularly known as *Harry the Fish Guy*, hammered it out in his book, *"Who Kidnapped Excellence?"*

1 Excellence is an inside-out proposition, which means that it starts with you.
2 You are in a race and then put in your best.
3 There is no second place for excellence, excellence is the goal – you are either moving towards it or away from it.
4 All five qualities for attaining and maintaining excellence must be present such as passion, competency, communication, flexibility, and ownership.

Having a better understanding of the above four tenets of excellence would enable anyone to adopt the common sense in becoming whatever they choose to be. Excellence is always for and only on the side of those who take responsibility for their actions and do not blame others, those who never deceive to impress others, which is a way of pretending to know or understand. Excellence is about one knowing his or her brilliance, such as natural talent and also invests in the talent to make it a long-lasting success because there is a reward for such. Excellence implies striving for quality which requires setting higher standards for anyone in the right position for facing down challenges. There is no shortcut to

FACTS ABOUT EXCELLENCE

excellence or victory, the work just needs to be done, no doubt about it, it is about being committed towards the desired passion. It implies the willingness to carry on without thinking of any form of reward. Commitment drives and anchors people during challenging times. It also enables us to maintain a high degree of perseverance. Commitment opens the door to self-mastery and excellence. Another fact in attaining excellence is the ability to observe and maintain growth because it enables one to note when progress is made. You are given an opportunity to record discovery in terms of implementing new strategies and plans in attaching more clients and customers, developing new skills and a culture of change via training, coaching, and mentoring.

Behavioral change is often required in most cases to achieve excellence. This cannot be neglected, striving for excellence usually means that people need to change their behavior. Changing behavior entails sustained effort. Creating the right environment to achieve excellence requires leaders who provide strong support. It is paramount for leaders to recognize the current performance of their team and encourage them to do more, and motivate them to carry on with effective performance.

Maintaining and sustaining whatever is being achieved is the best way to live and leave a legacy. Achieving success in an endeavor is wonderful but having a good significance is better. There is also establishing a leadership culture that provides and retains one's vision and purpose in fostering a high level of performance. The most important thing about achieving success is to contribute positively to the world around us by showing and motivating others on how to courageously leave their comfort zone. Authentic leaders are well known for constantly building their legacies by involving everyone around them in being committed towards quality. Involvement is also a way of adding value to them because leadership is more than being a leader. It is about delivering expected results in breaking limitations and fulfilling missions as this is the best way to maintain and sustain excellence. Maintaining and sustaining success help leaders or anyone in reaching and making sound decisions in complex and unpredictable environments and achieving sustainable results via effective communication.

When maintaining and sustaining success or an outstanding leadership when creating a lasting legacy, it is paramount to remain committed to the values of justice and caring for others. For example, Angelina Jolie-Pitt, the American actress, filmmaker, and humanitarian is well known for her campaign against sexual violence in military conflict zones by the British government, for which she received many awards and recognitions for her humanitarian work. She was the first recipient of the Citizen of the World Award by the United Nations Correspondents Association. She was awarded the Global Humanitarian Award by the UNA-USA in October 2005, and she received the Freedom Award from the International Rescue Committee in November 2007. Her legacy has made a huge impact and benefited many people. The impact of her work will be read by many in years to come. Acting from a strong self-concept to start with; self-concept is a factual description of what and how one perceives one's self, it is about the rate at which one sees and believes in himself or herself. If anyone sees his or her as a negative figure, the individual would always experience having the feeling of being a failure before taking action and also having the fear of facing challenges, uncertainties, and taking risks, which makes anyone remain the same regardless of the change in time. Maintaining and sustaining excellence involve thinking critically and acting creatively to articulate a positive sense of direction, risks willingly and wisely towards attaining an outstanding service. Maintaining and sustaining

FACTS ABOUT EXCELLENCE

is about recognizing one's internal values which makes one believe in himself and remain fearless in meeting expectations and demands of various stakeholders.

One major habit of excellent people is the ability to review their past successes or performances and also preview or predict future successes of their strategy and resources. In predicting future successes, it is paramount to balance the value for both internal and external stakeholders. In sustaining there is a huge need to avoid arrogance because it is a guaranteed way to never achieve and sustain excellence. If achieved, this person would end up losing all at a certain point in time. Never a good thing, being arrogant means *know it all, can do* or *make it without others* and *I have got all answers.*

In building and sustaining excellence, it is essential to stick to one's purpose and to focus on it as this would reflect where to invest energy and activity to avoid distractions and confusion. The more focused a person is, the more a person is able to achieve visions and objectives, attain goals, improve performance, facilitate innovation and taking risks intelligently. Never allow anyone to stop you from achieving your dreams or purpose in life, due to their past failures or previous negative experiences. Bear in mind, the same way they are responsible for their failure, the same way you would be responsible for yours. If you dare to follow or take to their ill advice, this could make you stagnant or subject you to limitations. In attaining, maintaining and sustaining excellence, there is a need for the intellectual growth to have taken place in order to be able to view situations from an imaginary distance with a trained sight and realistic manner before taking steps. To be clear, excellence is not a matter of rushing to acquire material items or being in a haste to meet up with other peers on a competitive ground or a particular level, these are all temporal. However, it is all about abiding by the right principles and applying the right knowledge in laying a solid foundation towards living an unlimited life and lasting legacy. I desire and consider excellence paramount because I see it as the courageous ability to step outside one's comfort zone, training with a spirit of endeavor, and accepting the inevitability of trials and tribulations for the expectation of a platinum crown. To draw the curtain on how to attain, maintain and sustain excellence, leaders need to ensure others and do their best while leading in a respectful and responsible manner.

To hit the nail on the head, attaining excellence is never a matter of doing things for the sake of it. Rather, it is a matter of getting things done with an accurate insight as mentioned in the seven principles of transformation. It requires a deep insight to understand and recognize the impact and value to carry out an outstanding performance in any situation. It is also not an issue of *'I can play all roles'*, reflecting a selfish mindset acting as a jack-of-all- trades, master of none. Excellence could only be achieved in an organization, team, and relationship if engaged with other diligent and competent people. Those with the right mindset know best where to give the right advice and support in making one's dreams and desires become a reality. The twice Formula One World Champion, Lewis Hamilton, was reported to have approached the McLaren Team Principal Ron Dennis about his desire to race for the team at the age of ten. In respect to the number of times he has won the race championship o far, his journey towards excellence started from the day he desired to race for McLaren. Obviously, it required him to learn and understand the right skills to become a Formula One driver via the impact of effective training and coaching towards developing a focused mindset in achieving his goal. It also required him to engage himself with the right people such as his father who manages him, McLaren, the company that chose to invest in him, and other teammates who support him in ensuring that all things are in good condition for him to participate in any racing event. It took someone like Ron Dennis to discover and see the golden potentials in Lewis Hamilton before signing him to the team. The president of the International Association of Athletics Federations (IAAF), Sebastian Newbold Coe, known as Lord Coe, was able to attain heights in his athletic career as a result of diligence and consistency. Thanks to his achievements, he was able to venture into politics and become a Member of Parliament for Falmouth and Camborne. Later he chaired the 2012 London Olympics and was also able to become the president of the International Association of Athletics Federations. Despite losing his seat in the 1997 British general election, he was still able to make waves at different levels and was still recognized as an icon in the British sports history. He was dedicated to what he loved doing the most and how to do best, *'All my life I have loved sports!'* He was even mentioned at the opening ceremony of the London 2012 Olympic Games. Tracing his history, he was focused and committed to maintaining a performance towards achieving more of whatever he could do during his prime because he understood the importance of time and opportunities. Without the engagement of his father, Percy Newbold "Peter" Coe, he might not have been able to attain as much in his career. The fact remains, I am yet to come across a leader, champion or any distinguished person who made milestones without engaging others. Watching the popular British television chat show, *Life Stories*, hosted by Piers Morgan, the successful stories of various celebrity guests reflect the benefits of excelling in any particular field and how most celebrities grew from grass to grace. One common factor I have to realize is that they all worked and dedicated themselves at the right time, which is the hidden treasure of any delightful person, no alternative or excuses about the point. It is either you help meet their expectations and get paid for it or you ditch it. Bear in mind that someone of lesser potential or values might carry on from where you stopped, complete the project, and get the whole credit for the job that was initiated and begun by you. The major facts I like every reader to take on board is the need and understanding that the mysteries of excellence discussed in this book could also be regarded as the applicable principles and relevant facts in a raw state. These consist of the in-depth truth regarding excelling beyond limitation because they could be proved beyond reasonable doubt in terms of standing the test of value, reality and time. However, the realities of excellence remain unchangeable and it requires knowing your passion before understanding it. It is a matter of learning from the best to have a perfect insight of gathering, the required intelligence towards embracing professionalism and managing resources effectively. Desiring excellence requires one to be of a progressive mind to enable them to strive for peak results, which are a major parameter in creating a lasting and positive impact. In reality, attaining excellence is the major step before recognition; i.e. standing before kings.

KNOWING YOUR PASSION

"I've been absolutely terrified every moment of my life and I've never let it keep me from doing a single thing that I wanted to do". — Georgia O'Keefe

Knowing one's passion is a major key for anyone to be fulfilled in life, without knowing it, the case is similar to that soldier at the warfront and still wondering why he is there or waiting to ask what's going on in the war zone. However, a confused man is a lost man because simple direction becomes his headache. To avoid being a confused person and living a meaningless life, one needs to know his specific passion that answers the reason for his existence. It is clear from the situation that the soldier had no passion for his job and can never be fulfilled while still in the army, making positive contributions in defeating his nation or going further in his military career. It is easy to say such a person found himself in the army unexpectedly. My fact is most people venture into careers, business, and other endeavors without having a passion for it and later put out sharing a negative experience mostly with the younger generations that might mislead them in terms of which direction to flow or not. It would be very rare to make a positive and meaningful contribution in any endeavor without being passionate about its success. The million dollar question is if a confused soldier was to lead others as a commander, what a disastrous movie to be watched by many? Knowing your passion creates and gives you a clear sense of direction and picture of what you want to do and where you want to be at a particular desired time.

Also, knowing how best to support others around you make you better than the current situation offers. Knowing your passion is not a matter of doing anything simply because you are in control or you are not accountable to anyone. Rather, it is about operating in a specific direction with a clear insight because the more you know your passion, the higher your tendency of attaining excellence in your field. It is not a matter of grabbing an opportunity due to smartness or common doors being opened by any government or non-governmental organizations. Your passion is something that needs to be well known, understood and considered vital. Knowing your passion is a major key to excellence once being backed up by the required enthusiasm.

Many believe and see passion as anything that brings in a lot of money or enables you to live in mansions of various sizes in the world largest cities. The fact is such people are yet to discover themselves in a consistent manner. A former schoolmate of mine had the passion for training children in how to play football but instead went for a career that was influenced by the success of a friend and his money. Six years later, he discovered that wasn't meant for him because he found it difficult to focus on his job. Whenever he saw a nearby youth team training after school hours through the window, he later admitted he wasn't fulfilling his purpose because he found himself being stuck, on the verge of failing. His manager decided to change his seat but still, he would get up unknowingly to watch those young stars. Moreover, he loved to discuss and analyze football with everyone in the office but seemed to be an odd-ball because not everyone in the office loved football. Everyone knew he was passionate about this sport, but he left without making an impact because

KNOWING YOUR PASSION

the job wasn't his passion and later trained to become a football coach. In our discussion a few years ago, he considered those years wasted. That is due to the fact that he was never fulfilled spending six years working in the city and made his way up in his coaching career speedily because of the passion he had for what he was doing. You may be one of those who hasn't identified their passion, I suggest you sit and study yourself to discover who you are, what you stand for and what the positive minded one's around you know about you to discover your uniqueness.

At this point, it is pivotal to define what passion is, provided we now understand it is not all about money but the burning light within that enables our inner force to become active in creating a positive impact and lasting legacy.

WHAT IS PASSION?

The dictionary defines passion as "having a keen enthusiasm or intense desire for something." The positive descriptions include such words as fervent, zealous, obsessive, and fanatical. A passion is a calling in one's life which one might grow up knowing or had been discovered at one point or the other. Passion could be discovered through one's talent or personal development in which others could help us with. Many do say they are not sure of where to start. These people need to seek the right advice and learn from the best, a topic that will be later discussed in this book.

Donovan Bailey, a retired Canadian sprinter who made waves in the track and field championships in the mid 90's, once said:

> "Follow your passion, be prepared to work hard and sacrifice, and, above all, and don't let anyone limit your dreams".

THE MYSTERIES OF EXCELLENCE

In reality, knowing your passion is not sufficient in attaining excellence as it requires knowing what your dreams are, the work to be done alongside with the right time and the sacrifice to be made to make your story worth telling. Taking insight from Donovan Bailey's quote, some intelligent and powerful statements were combined in his quote: *follow your passion*. It is wise for anyone desiring excellence to follow their passion with curiosity and not making money their primary consideration or major motive. The act of following your passion with curiosity enables you to remain excited about your life and eventually makes your life meaningful. Many write-ups do claim that following your passion is bad advice but I ask, how can anyone attain excellence doing something they never loved or something they had no call for. The soldier previously mentioned was confused because he had no calling or conviction to defend his country. He may go miles if policing his local community but staging at the warfront wasn't his passion. The issue is, it is either they don't know what passion is or they do but don't know what else needs to be done to make their passion active. I can't imagine the depth of negative impact or influence such writers could be making on the younger generation and to those who desire to change direction or attain excellence in their endeavors. One major secret of excellence is to follow your passion and success will follow at various stages once the required work is done. If anyone does whatever he or she is passionate about, no matter what the fact might be, excuses can never hold such a person down because of the burning desire to make their vision a reality. King Solomon said in the Book of Proverbs 18:16, *"a man's gift makes way for him"*. 'The question is, how can a gift that is not yours make way for you? Secondly, what is a gift? In simple terms, a gift would be referred to as a natural ability or talent. In reality, following your passion would always enable the right support

KNOWING YOUR PASSION

to come your way, because no one would like to invest in something they are not good at as it would eventually end up being a waste of time and resources. My neighbor, Mrs. Janet Smith, in our conversation, a few years back, promised to drive her daughters down for swinging classes every weekend because she discovered it was their passion from their young age. So she chose not to waste her time and money by forcing them to become singers or actresses. Her role in supporting them in following their passion would make them excel in the future.

Following your passion shows how realistic you are and it will distinguish you from the crowd in the long run. Knowing and following your passion would always help in boosting the level of your confidence as in improving your ability towards getting to the top, no matter the struggle, time or age, you can never be disappointed by whatever you are passionate about. Knowing your passion will reflect your core values, principles, and beliefs that you live and stand by. Another benefit of following your passion is that it enables you to know and understand your hobbies. However, knowing your core values and hobbies positions you on the path to excellence because it shows you are diligent in every way. The fact remains, a lizard can never become an alligator, finding and knowing your passion is not about pretending to be someone else or something you are not and can never be, the best way to excel and create a positive impact is to be yourself and do whatever good thing you love doing.

Another fact to be considered in Donovan Bailey's quote is *"be prepared to work"*. This means that just knowing your passion is not sufficient for you to excel as mentioned earlier on. Instead, you need to be doing the required job. This is what adds value and meaning to anything worth doing as humans. Many know their passion and never walk towards it, the same was the story of the talents in the (Matthew 25:14-

THE MYSTERIES OF EXCELLENCE

30), in which a master who was about to travel gave talents to his three servants and went his way. The third servant had a nonchalant attitude and also an act of irresponsibility in which disallowed him from facing the reality and challenges in meeting the master's expectations. It was so easy for the third to fail in meeting the master's expectations because he wasn't passionate about his future, *"talk less of what was given to him in which taught him to have invested with bankers to have more"*. Likewise, knowing and following your passion is a good investment in your talents to add more of your own to make it abundant. Another unforgettable lesson in that passage was the master considered the servant worthless and later decided to cast him into the outer darkness. Lewis Hamilton knew his passion at a young age and worked towards it and later stood among the world legends of car racing. The statement *"be prepared to work"* requires an unbeatable determination in giving whatever it takes in getting to the peak of the mountain top. It also means focusing on your heart's desire(s) and not giving up on your goals no matter the setbacks or disappointments. *"Be prepared to work"* also means having the initiative and courage to take the right action at the right time and adding momentum towards finishing those tasks. These tasks are considered to be hard and necessary, performed by you, and not have you waiting or expecting others to do it for you. Bear in mind, others would only give you what they have and tell you what they want you to know and not what you want or need to know. The statement also means facing your fears and battling doubts by having a positive attitude in tough situations. To hit home, it means making mistakes, falling down, or suffering embarrassment or disappointment from loved ones; to never fail or attaining the peak of one's desire but learning from these experiences including that of others and using them to push forward towards your goal. Donovan

KNOWING YOUR PASSION

Bailey did mention in his quote the word *sacrifice*. Taking insight from the dictionary, the word *sacrifice* literally means to give up something of personal value or interest for the sake of other considerations, to abandon something of pleasure for a reason, to surrender in expectation of a particular significance, to forego something of importance, to forfeit something of value for a loved one. No man makes a sacrifice for no reason or in expectation of nothing. However, knowing your passion requires you knowing what sacrifices need to be made and the significance of what you desire to achieve at the end of a specific term. I am sure for sportsmen such as Usain Bolt and Lionel Messi, to remain fit and excel in the sporting world, they would have sacrificed having some fatty meals and other diets. And the last part of Donovan Bailey's quote *'and, above all, and don't let anyone limit your dreams.'* To back up his statement, the says Timothy 4:12, *"let no man despise your youth"*. In reality, let no man kill your passion or dream as in regard to the calling in which you stand for and make you do something else which you have no passion for or have no reason do it. A youthful stage is a prime time where one could plan effectively and achieve the best of one's desire, it's the best time to lay track for one's overall success in life. The fact is, once the youthful stage is wasted or exchanged for porridge like of Esau, the level of struggle increases. To make a reasonable impact on your passion, your mentality and motive need to be the right one, many venture into policies to fight for the right of the masses, while some do for the sake of enriching themselves, they pretend to serve the public where in fact they dominate and enslave the public. The fact they end up failing and their offspring never attain their heights are due to their preteens and record. Keeping relationships with negative or immature minded people makes you see your passion with contempt, which in turn makes you disregard those actions that need to be considered to help you make your dream a reality. According to Dr. Mike Murdock, in his book, 1001 Wisdom Keys, key 325 states, *"those who cannot Increase you will inevitably decrease you"*. He went ahead in specifying various ways of gathering and the need to belong to those groups that would enable you to keep your passion alive and help make your dream a reality.

As far as you know, whatever it is that you are passionate about, all you need to do is to remain consistent in developing and preparing yourself for opportunities ahead which might serve as platforms towards doing greatness. Someone telling or keeping you below your limitations without telling you how to increase your strength has nothing good for you in his store. However, it is advisable you check the next step. In fact, even if advice seems to be good for you, it doesn't mean it is the best for you. This is similar to the agricultural science teacher or tutor who tells the students to plant their crops during the rainy season in order to harvest at a particular period. Conversely, the students are not told to remove the weeds before planting or to revisit their farmland to remove the weeds while the crops are growing to enable the crops to have sufficient nutrients to grow as expected. Such a tutor is not preparing his students for a good harvest because the inaccurate information would end up limiting the students' performance in terms of their outputs during harvest. Likewise, anyone not advising you on how to achieve your dream, mostly regarding steps that need to be taken or any required sacrifice, would kill your dream if not cared for. One unchangeable fact about passion is that it is inspirational and not a physical commodity that can be purchased for a specified amount. Once it is gone, the case becomes similar to a car without an engine. Another major reason why you need to be sure of the potential results of your passion is that there is advice everywhere and everyone around you will always have something to tell and a story to back it up with. Whether

KNOWING YOUR PASSION

the story is counterfeit or genuine, without knowing what you are aiming at boosts your confidence and keeps the passion in you alive. However, it is your main responsibility in finding the right advice that fits you, or else the wrong ones would always lead to a setback or stagnancy. Another fact is whoever succeeds in misleading you with wrong advice regarding your passion would never take the blame, nor would they compensate you for failure because life itself is about productivity and not excuses. Knowing your passion is worthwhile and therefore it needs to be cherished because as humans we never value what we have until we lose it.

Ella Fitzgerald, the late Queen of Jazz, once said,

> "Just don't give up trying to do what you really want to do. Where there's love and inspiration, I don't think you can go wrong".

To clear the air, there's no way you can understand your purpose in life without knowing what it is and there's no way to excel in any endeavor once you have given up. The young man who desires the golden egg covers it up with rocks for the purpose of marrying the king's daughter. He would surely consider inspecting the cutting edge of the ax given to him, whether it was old or new because he could be passionate about the opportunity before him which could change his life for the better, if only he fulfilled the task or he could make his life stagnant if giving up halfway. For other positive-minded people around to see a vision and reality in whatever you are trying to do, you need to see the light in it first. Seeing the light makes it easier to gain their people's attention, support and inspiration which in turn gives you the courage to carry on, regardless of the trials and errors. However, most people do see errors as a failure and give up more than an opportunity to learn and try again. Love and inspiration from the right people will always help you to discover and light up your passion and also turns up the power within you to take the right action. The undeniable fact is that support and inspiration wipe away fears in anyone because they are both end products of being courageous.

In knowing your passion, there is a huge need to remain consistent in whatever your passion might be at any point in time. This is the fact that distinguishes the good from the best. The more consistent you are, the more inspired you become to create something new that requires making continuous research and practice regardless of the inconvenience. Just as Mohammed Ali said, he hated all the time he spent training but said to himself *'don't quit.'* The truth is that boxing was his passion and he needed to be consistent in practice ahead of every match he faced in order to bring out the best in him. Other boxers in his career days were also good but something made him the best. Not placing money as the reason behind your passion would enable you to go above and beyond expectations and limitations. However, no obstacle should stop you from achieving gradual success leading towards excellence. Knowing your passion is the first step to excel in life and in any endeavor because it is the origin of fulfillment having to abide by the necessary and accepted principles of excellence while not going off course. It makes you unstoppable while driving and aiming at your purpose with clarity, regardless of the sacrifices to be made. To hit home, knowing your passion enables you to live a value-based life which increases the light and inspiration in others, it enables others to desire excellence and give it whatever it takes. It enables you to create a positive impact on the lives of many, whether far or near. Bear in mind that attaining excellence is never an easy task, but it is a valuable one, and the more you avoid distraction and procrastination the quicker you will attain it.

KNOWING YOUR PASSION

The popular children presenter and television personality, Justin Fletcher, a.k.a. Mr. Tumble, knew his passion right from the time he was a student and was inspired by Phillip Schofield. However, he had gone miles in positively impacting the lives of children including mine. Edward, my son, loved him from eleven-months-old and took his finger and touched his nose when Mr. Tumble said to do. Other children presenters and television personalities such as Catherine Sandion, Andy Day, Pui Fan Lee and Sidney Sloane all knew their passion from when they were children from the way they act tirelessly. Many years ago, I applied for a customer service role, having passed the first stage of the interview, I was invited to the second stage that required an applicant going out with one of the trainee managers, who would later recommend an applicant for the job. I discovered the trainee manager who was assigned to me was passionate about things such as going door-to-door, trying to find funds for various charities and was ready to walk the whole town of London tirelessly. However, I was bored of going up and down buildings within various estates, stopping people at various bus stops and train stations. I couldn't see a future in it for myself and began to feel pains all over my body. This pushed me to ask if there would be any break and the closing, "Oh, I don't think of having breaks and we close at 21: 00 hours, any problem with that?" he asked. "Oh, it's okay by me," I replied. "At around 14: 50", while I looked at my watch, the thoughts were swirling around my mind. Was there a future in this job for me? Am I passionate about this job? Can I afford to be doing a job I am not passionate about for longer hours? Plus the wages depended on the number of signings I got and how they are donated regularly. In less than five minutes I knew the job wasn't for me so I called the trainee manager and called it a day because I knew no matter how long I carried on with the job I wouldn't be fulfilled .

THE MYSTERIES OF EXCELLENCE

A young man, while carrying out his street cleaning job, saw a bus driving vacancy and was passionate about it. He went into the office and made an inquiry on how to fill out an application. He met with one of the directors who asked him if he had gotten a driving license, "Oh, I thought I would be trained," he responded to the director's question. "Of course, we train people to become bus drivers but you must hold at least a year-old driving license," the director replied. "Okay", the young man replied. "I now know what to do, thank you, sir!" The young man left and carried on with his job. Two months later, while the director was driving, he happened to pass the particular young man who waved at him and showed his driving license. The director was delighted and told the young man to visit him in his office to fill out an application form. Three months later while the young man was carrying out his job, as usual, he received a phone call from the director to start the training, "Sir, my license is less than six months old", he responded. "Oh, I am aware of that", the director replied, "and I have gotten a copy of it with here with me. If you are ready please start the training next week!" And that's how he got his passionate job without an interview and in less time than he expected. The director had every reason to bend the rules simply because of the fact that the young man's passion and ability to take action once he had gotten the required information showed initiative. The director knew he was hiring someone who dearly wanted the job. The bottom line is once you know your passion in life, others will see it in you as well and those who support you would have known where and how to help you. Knowing your passion is the wisdom behind you not living another man's life because people venture into various endeavors wrongly due to someone else's media popularity and periodic wealth without understanding the person's calling and sacrifice before attaining greatness. The fact is, if another man begins to have the desire to succeed in the wrong direction, he might be lucky in a few cases, but also might end up regretting it after having negative experiences. Attaining excellence is a matter of abiding by reasonable and relevant principles, such as planting the right seed in the right soil at the right time to experience a bountiful harvest.

UNDERSTANDING YOUR PASSION

"When you're surrounded by people who share a passionate commitment around a common purpose, anything is possible".

-Howard Schultz

Knowing your passion and understanding it is two different things. Knowing it is about having the right idea of what and where you want to be and at looking at a particular future while understanding it gives the right insight as in how to make your passion a reality. In a nutshell, knowing your passion is about what you want to be and why, while understanding your passion is about how to be a concept that goes along with the attitude of creating a possibility platform to make it be. Knowing one's passion and not understanding it is the major reason talented people are unable to fulfil their visions and live their dreams. The lack of understanding in any good intention makes people see simple and necessary steps with complexity and as huge challenges which therefore make the mission become impossible. Nothing else would have enabled talented people to beat the limitations or obstacles that determined their faith and go beyond expectations other than understanding one's calling. The unchangeable fact is no matter how talented a man or woman may be, where they stand determines who they see and what

UNDERSTANDING YOUR PASSION

they get as a result of the available opportunities in any given situation. Standing in the right place at the right time requires understanding your passion. Understanding your passion gives and increases your probability of excelling. Understanding your passion enables you to know the best advice to take and how best to apply it. Any advice given by anyone regardless of their age, experience, and previous achievement must be weighed carefully because the time and situations change constantly and the best drink of yesterday might be the worst of all drinks today. Bear in mind there is a huge need to be sure of the ability and achievements of your advisor or mentor, because how can someone without a business advise you on how to run yours? Ideas might count but someone with the in-depth practical experience would always be the best person to approach before making any move. Lack of proper understanding of your passion would make it easier to lose your vision and walk away from your calling and struggling for that which is not yours. Understanding your passion enables you to expand the intellectual ability to rise above limitations because the more you understand it, the more equipped and empowered you to become in facing challenges fearlessly. Understanding your passion enables you to count all joy by seeing the light within yourself and others, regardless of the current unpleasant and disappointing situations you might be facing. Nothing else makes one an authority in any field more than understanding the field itself and knowing what it takes to go that extra mile in that same field. Understanding your passion enables you to be more significant in terms of what you have to offer others. In fulfilling your purpose in life, you must know the reason why you need to be committed to becoming successful in your endeavour. You also need to create your uniqueness in whatever you do regardless of the number of people doing the same thing. The major reason why only a few become distinguished in more aspects of their life is simply because they have the mindset in making things possible where others are thinking of giving up. Bear in the mind that their mindset is always a result of understanding their passion and this makes them unstoppable in attaining heights. However, they are seen as agents of change because they are not moved by the fear of the unknown or poor outcomes at previous stages of any process. They are confident of their values and what they can do in creating a positive change. Taking insight from the book *Failing Forward* by John C. Maxwell, I was able to comprehend that anyone who understands his passion and core values would always overcome failure and become the kind of achiever he or she has always wanted to be, it was just a matter of time and not by magic. Nelson Mandela once said, *"there is no passion to be found playing small, in settling for a life that is less than one you are capable of living"*. The only thing that can enable a man never to settle for less in life is the ability to understand himself, passion and vision. Without these attributes, the case is similar to a train without a direction. Part of the lessons I learned from reading the book *Failing Forward* is that failing in one thing is not failing in all things. Likewise, experiencing difficulty at a particular point in one's life doesn't mean one is a total failure. I do remember becoming a master in a job I once found very difficult while thinking of quitting the job for another, I decided to learn the right skills I needed to understand. A few weeks later, I became the master of it for a long time. Another lesson I learned from reading the same book was that failure is a necessary part of growing up because life itself is based on and filled with trials and errors, in which it only requires a man of wisdom to scale through. Without understanding what the principal thing is, the story would always be like the house built on sand which could not stand the test of the rain and wind. The best business and life coaches are those who have recorded failures at one point in their lives. Keep in mind, making mistakes or recording failures would never disvalue you as a human being, provided you have the courage and insight to realize and learn from them and improve. According to John C. Maxwell's terminology, "fail forward," I learned from each mistake I have ever made and consider myself better by waxing stronger in beating my fears and facing down challenges by thinking fast of what to do next. He writes: *"One of the greatest problems people have with failure is that they are too quick to judge isolated situations in their lives and label them as failures"*. Rather than thinking and capitalizing on previous failures or allowing people to keep on reminding you of your errors, keep the bigger picture in mind and persevere with the right situation for a genuine reason. Know that your ability to wait could be regarded as a waste of time by others, but use this time to think creatively. Don't let failure kill your vision and passion within you or limit you in any way. John C. Maxwell's message was clear as he writes the seven key abilities that allow successful people to fail forward instead of taking each setback personally. Successful people:

1 Never accept rejection. Rather, if they reject it, face the challenges of moving forward, having understood your core values and passion is paramount to take control of negative situations. Learn those things which are necessary and take the full responsibility of making the right decision at the right time. Avoid being taken for granted in the name of humility and always be on the alert to fight and strive for golden movements. In rejecting rejections, never project negative conversations onto future possibilities and never allow your mind to anchor your negative

experiences and never think of fighting the last battles. However, successful people don't blame themselves when they fail. They take responsibility for each setback, and they don't take the failure personally.

2   Always see and view failure as temporary and not something that should determine your future. People who personalize failure see a problem as a hole they're permanently stuck in, while achievers see any predicament as temporary, placing aside previous disappointment, failure, and errors and focus on a better tomorrow.

3   View each failure as an isolated incident and consider it as an avenue to discover the required keys and step forward. Successful people don't define themselves by individual failures and they never consider their last card played at any point in time. They recognize that each setback is a small part of the whole.

4   Have realistic expectations. Success needs to be prepared for because it takes time and does not occur by magic. When you pursue anything worthwhile, there are going to be bumps along the way. However, expectations need to be worthwhile in terms of achieving them as one needs to be realistic in his aspirations and visions for the future by assessing outcomes at various stages and identifying barriers and patterns for improvements. Anyone or any leaders aiming at excellence needs to be realistic in their level of commitment and motivation in carrying others along and need to have the required support and information to make life easier, mostly during transformational periods.

UNDERSTANDING YOUR PASSION

5. Focus on strengths and not weaknesses. Focus on leveraging and amplifying your strengths which allows you to multiply your results. Fix any fatal weakness as fast as possible and do not disallow you from reaching your goals. This attitude will open the door to productivity and enables you to experience faster growth and development.
6. Consider various approaches to getting things done. For example, always consider an alternative when the unexpected happens, such as a delay or breakdown occurs. From experience, most people who gave up and made their story not worthwhile are those who suffered a delay or a breakdown and could not turn things around by not thinking of what needed to be done next. "Achievers are willing to vary their approaches to problems, "Maxwell writes. "That's important in every walk of life, not just business." If one approach doesn't work for you, if it brings repeated failure, then try something else. Maxwell is saying that to fail forward, you must do what works for you, not necessarily what works for other people.
7. Believe in bouncing back. Successful people are resilient; they never allow an error to keep them down. They learn from their mistakes and move on.

The truth is, without being sure of your passion and understanding it, you might find it difficult to apply the above terminologies because it is not a one-cap-fits-all process. Obtaining the right cap for the right head, you need to discover yourself in relationship to the situation you are facing before applying any principle. Having understood your passion, it becomes necessary to follow your path. In fact, by knowing your calling, you increase the positive impact you intend to create in the lives of others. By so doing you would be enjoying the process of "doing" more or "getting" a flash of insight. Another point is to seek ways of motivating yourself to remain committed to your part on the path to excellence. To clear the air, sports are a specific direction which enabled people to fulfil their destiny. However, sporting has many branches such as boxing, football, badminton, cycling, and much more. Understanding your passion enables you to utilize your strength and makes you stronger at aiming and meeting high-performance standards because it is an expectation of any successful person. Your passion would enable you to make meaningful progress in addition to your satisfaction and happiness having been fulfilled. Your passion opens the door to creativity because the right ideas and inspiration come to the right person on the right field at the right time. A better understanding of your passion would always enable you to navigate through life and to tap into more happiness, joy, and fulfillment in any endeavor. Having true passion requires you to be doing something that is in line with your life purpose and allowing you to use your personal strengths. Many positive things happen where passion dwells because it brings energy to carry on tirelessly, it creates a positive environment for things to be done with little or no interruption, it drives vision towards being realistic, it increases influence and ignites others to act at the right time and not be left out. Passion brings better opportunities and opens the door to success by creating the possibility for positive change.

Understanding your passion increases your sense of direction in living a purposeful life. It is never about seeking a loophole in attaining cheap popularity, nor is it a platform for playing or blending rules secretly in making your way to the top because a high rise laid on a watery foundation would

UNDERSTANDING YOUR PASSION

never stand the test of quality and time. However, sticking to the top requires the ability to attain, maintain and sustain a good legacy which needs to build on the right and relevant principles to make a successful story worthwhile. Knowing and understanding your passion helps in building your internal knowledge that is an intellectual capital. This enables you to possess your knowledge as in how to run your business, career, and other aspects of your life. Another reason to know and understand your passion is the ability to enable, rightly direct others and enable them to grow. Understanding your passion enables you to play your expected role effectively. Let's take the game of soccer as an example: each player has a specific position with an expectation to meet. The goalkeeper is not expected to be seen in the box of the opponent in the aim of trying to score a goal else the risk might turn down the effort of others.

Operating a business that you are passionate about enables you to produce and deliver value and satisfaction to your customers because the money wouldn't be the most important thing. Knowing and going for whatever is yours is the lifestyle anyone is expected to live. Excellence is a legacy and worth understanding before attaining. Your passion would enable you to attain greatness if the required work is done at the right time and at the right place with wisdom, there wouldn't be the need to force things to happen. Knowing your passion and sitting on the fence would never bring the best out of you or make you a radiating light to others. The stays in Luke 8:16:

> "No man, when he hath lighted a candle, covereth it with a vessel, or putteth it under a bed; but setteth it on a candlestick, that they which enter in may see the light".

THE MYSTERIES OF EXCELLENCE

Knowing it alone can't enable you to create a positive impact on others. However, understanding your passion would enable you to take the right action towards recording excellence by placing the candlestick at the right place. To sum it up, passion is the only thing that enables you to catch your vision and enables you to embark on the strategic mission towards making you relevant and of particular significance in fulfilling your destiny and living your dream. The ability to understand your passion creates the platform to discover, develop, manage and effectively utilize your skills and other forms of resources to achieve your dreams. Lack of understanding has made many people in their lifetime ignorantly embrace sentiment and pretense that made them a waste to themselves and bonus to others. Understanding is the first step towards giving a solution in any challenging situation and enabling one to make a fortune from one's passion due to the huge insight which understanding gives. The most dangerous situation to come across in life is to be led by a leader without understanding because the empathy and insight to influence and carry others would be lacking and such leaders would eventually be myopic in all they do. The richest man that ever lived, King Solomon, made it clear in the Proverbs 4:7, *"in all your getting's, get understanding"*. Without beating around the bush, understanding facilitates growth and maturity in making consistent strides towards miles in any direction. It requires a deep level of understanding to know that facing down challenges and moving on courageously is better than being stagnant and limited joyfully which is always a result of ignorance. Applying understanding in one's passion is an example of well-doing, and as it says in the book of Galatians 6:9,

"let's not be weary in well-doing, for in due time we will reap a harvest if we do not give up".

UNDERSTANDING YOUR PASSION

Understanding your passion makes you more creative and realistic in building your distinguished legacy. Therefore, knowing and understanding your passion is never a light matter. Commitment and continuation in developing and investing in various initiatives are the two major keys in recording progression at various levels. In fact, it says in Ecclesiastes 11:6,

"Sow your seed in the morning, and at evening let your hands not be idle, for you do not know which will succeed, whether this or that, or whether both will do equally well".

Apart from knowing and understanding your passion, there is always a huge need to be sensitive and intelligent in channeling things the right way to keep you fully prepared ahead of golden opportunities because everyone who comes across luck ends up being lucky. However, understanding your passion facilitates the ability to identify and choose the right people to discuss plans and work with because the says Amos 3:3:

"Can two walk together, except they be agreed?"

In reality, having a concrete agreement(s) towards fulfilling a purpose is always an end product of proper understanding.

"Once upon a time" is the beginning of every story and *"only if I'd known"* is the conclusion of every regrettable situation. According to King Solomon in the understanding is paramount to the way we think before taking action which reflects on us as being intelligent or a novice, proper understanding enables a man to make a fortune from his passion or talent. Lack of understanding could make a man

fail at his attempts and remain stagnant all his lifetime because understanding creates the platform for insights and later creates the platform for direction. From experience, some public speakers are more inspirational and productive than others due to their various levels of understanding regarding a particular topic. Their ability to practice the basic skills of public speaking such as planning appropriately, engaging with the audience to make one's message meaningful, thinking positively before speaking and paying attention to body language is also a learned advantage. In a nutshell, understanding is a basic necessity for the way we live which improves our lives and the way we relate to others and also how we handle and solve complex situations. Many people spend their lifetime trying to please others and not discovering and understanding themselves, while some understood the rudiments of their direction and not the mysteries, which is the major reason they were never fulfilled in any endeavor. According to T.D. Jakes, the American pastor:

> "Destiny means understanding your destination, in reality, the need for understanding is vital before attaining greatness in any aspect of one's life".

However, understanding could only be given by the right people and not just the good ones, take it or leave it. You being in the midst of twenty wrong people is just the same as being alone because none of them would be able to help you in getting to your right destination. In a few words, a man who doesn't understand his destination is on the road to nowhere and is on the platform of becoming irrelevant.

LEARNING FROM THE BEST

"Learn from yesterday, live for today, hope for tomorrow. The important thing is not to stop questioning."

-Albert Einstein

After addressing a group of young adults a few years ago, a young man, Benedict, came to my hotel room and expressed his fears.*"Sir, why do think most people start their life on the bright side of life and along the way can no longer move on and end up with their dreams unfulfilled?"* The fact is, he has learned from yesterday, which is a common occurrence in the lives of some people including celebrities. His hope for tomorrow is living a life free from dropping off the ladder unexpectedly, and this made him do the most important thing by questioning the situation ahead of the future. *"Have you seen a wise man depending on the fuel in the new car purchased and not replacing it after few days?* I asked him.*"The fuel in the new car is just to drive out of the showroom and a few miles more."* The reason why a man could start on the bright side and get stuck half way in fulfilling their destiny is because they depend so much on their previous education, training, and qualification. Most people stop learning the day they leave school, and they believe learning and education to be the same, which happens to be a big mistake. Education has to do with being equipped in a specific field. For example, if after studying business administration, I became passionate about practicing law or changing my career, I would need to get myself educated in law or any other field I wish to operate in. Education is about gaining the correct and required knowledge in *knowing how to*, such as an idea, while learning is about *showing how to*, an execution. However, learning is an all-life phenomenon, it goes beyond education. A newly employed chartered accountant still needs to be shown how things work and how to get things done in the corporate world in terms of how to apply discretion at the right time and place. This is what learning is despite the fact he had already acquired the proper knowledge to become a chartered accountant in school which is also known as education. The ability to learn from the best in any field would enable you to have the right insight as to how to work on yourself and change things all around for the best. One of the most common reasons people get paralyzed at one point in life is because they believe in traveling with high speed rather than understanding the direction they want to travel in. One thing they fail to realize is with every direction there are different parts and it requires proper learning to discover and step into the right part in any given direction at the right time. The fact is if anyone discovers his right direction and speeds on the wrong part, they would eventually get nowhere, no matter how well or early such a person starts. Studying a specific direction perfectly in terms of its requirements such as relevant skills and knowledge would enable anyone to have an idea of where to step at the right time and what to give up such as sacrifice to attain one's desire. If only the motorcyclist had studied the direction before accelerating, he would have known the proper speed he needed to control his bike at the dangerous junction, thus determining his position at the world class tournament and he would have made it to the end as the winner. The point is, speed is artificial and not the most important thing in life. It is only applicable where necessary and is not encouraged in all aspects of life. Another lesson while attaining a specific direction is the ability to equip oneself by updating your knowledge and skills in facing down challenges and making the best use of available opportunities. The inability to face down challenges has barred many people from advancing in their particular direction and likewise, determined faith in terms of what they were to able to achieve. The deep-rooted fact is that if a man is not well-equipped in terms of knowing what to do to attain a particular level and what to do next towards attaining even higher levels, one would end up being restricted from golden opportunities, no ifs, and's, or buts. Learning more about your direction increases your understanding of what it takes to progress with no limits and without alteration, it also enables you to see the light in yourself and in others by enabling you to know where best to support them and not mislead them. As a master coach and author, I still get coached by other coaches in my field.

Part of the lessons I have learned from successful people is the constant ability to pursue and maximize one's potentials through determination and focus on the major mysteries behind living a fulfilled life. To be fulfilled requires understanding your vision before executing a mission. A common mistake many people make is that they try to execute a mission before they understand the vision, and this makes the whole process meaningless. Having seen many successful people without a formal or proper education, I realized they were able to achieve greatness in their life because they were always thinking of attaining the next level which is a result of learning. Referring to Benedict's question, most people are unable to carry on at one point or the other simply because they prefer to settle for less due to previous experiences and the fear of the unknown. A young lady once discussed a brilliant idea of a book she wished to publish. After advising her on what to do and how to get things done, two years later, I met her at the arrival point at a local airport in London. I was shocked when she told me that she had stopped writing simply because her boss did not like seeing her write a book. It might seem to others in the office that she was not committed to her job. So, is that a clever idea? I asked why she did such a thing but she ran out of words. Just less than a year ago, the company went into administration and the same boss set up his company and could not consider her for employment. She made the decision of trying to please her boss at her own expense due to a lack of confidence and fear of what might happen if she wrote what she was passionate about. As a result, the message that she had for the world went untold. Successful people are never afraid of failure or taking action. Instead, they are always on the alert to give whatever it takes to reach the next level. I am sure from the discussion we had, writing that book would have turned her life around for the better. Unfortunately, she didn't have what it took to overcome the challenge of the mighty boss. She lost the vision of what she wanted to do as a result of a lack of determination and focus like many other people done. Knowing your challenge and not giving what it takes to overcome this hurdle and move to the next level would eventually keep one stagnant at the edge of success. According to the British novelist, J. K. Rowling who once said,

> "It is impossible to live without failing at something, unless you live so cautiously that you might as well not have lived at all – in which case, you fail by default."

LEARNING FROM THE BEST

In reality, the message is – don't fear failure at any point, always think and seek for the next alternative. If only the young lady had learned from someone who had previously experienced her same situation, this would have enabled her to know best on how to overcome the challenge. Learning from successful people would enable you to know how best to handle failures and mistakes because it might be a chance to learn more and improve as long as one keeps on trying with the right focus and determination. Failures in a particular area might require a change in direction in most cases.

In learning from the best, I discovered they are similar with having clear goals and they plan towards making their goals a reality. They don't work in their comfort zone but rather face challenges to obtain unlimited access to opportunity. Donald Trump, Warren Buffet, Bill Gates, and Oprah Winfrey are all successful because they are always striving towards the highest possible levels in their lives. One thing these successful people have in common is their ability to stand out from the crowd and grab any available opportunity that widens their coast. Learning from successful people would provide the right insight and tips which are extremely valuable in the pursuit of excellence. Rather than trying to learn everything from scratch, it is easier to follow the learning from others and build on it from there. This would jumpstart your learning curve by a huge degree. Dale Carnegie, one of the world's great writers, made it clear in order to excel, the way we think matters most;

> "The biggest lesson I have ever learned is the stupendous importance of what we think. If I knew what you thought, I would know what you are, for your thoughts make you what you are; by changing our thoughts we can change our lives".

THE MYSTERIES OF EXCELLENCE

Success is a key and a major step towards excellence which starts from within, meaning the way we think before taking action and not acting before thinking. Therefore, we can only give what we have.

Knowing and understanding how to build real and strategic relationships is a must. It is impossible to be successful without working well with others. Successful people show respect to others by listening and responding to ideas and criticism, and finding solutions in the interest of all concerned. Learning from the best in any field inspires you to embrace significance by not limiting yourself but being determined and focusing towards those great moments by keeping your eyes on the prize. Bill Gates once said that in order to win big, sometimes you have to take big risks, which means that the bigger your dream, the bigger your sacrifice, and commitment. One of the lessons from Donald Trump is the benefits of persistence that he refers to as the difference between success and failure. However, once a man has gotten to know and understand his passion, the next step is persistence which would eventually lead to his greatness in a matter of time. Donald Trump once said there are two sets of people, those who know what to do and never take action and those who take action once they know what to do. The reason why many lives go unfulfilled and many dreams are never realized is because most people had good visions, dreams, and wishes but never took the right action. I remember Mrs. Arida, a Senegalese, who broke out of limitation as a result of taking action in light of a golden opportunity. While speaking at a business start-up seminar in London, she told the story of how she accompanied her friends for a holiday job in the city of Touba in central Senegal. Getting to the construction site, she noticed the job as a result of the long-term government housing project which would last over four years. Mrs. Arida found the job too hard due to her slim stature, but she needed to provide funds for her university education. However, she discovered workers had to travel far to get their lunch and her mother happened to be a food seller. At the end of the day, while she was going to receive her wages, she approached the project manager and asked if she could supply food at lunch time for the workers realizing the problem experienced by everyone working at the site. The manager saw it as a brilliant idea and the issue was more critical for those working at night. *"Can you also supply us food by night?"* the manager asked. *"Of course, it's my job!"* she replied. Mrs. Arida from then on began supplying food twice a day without problems. Within time, she was introduced to other project managers and began to supply food on a larger scale by employing people to carry out various activities on her behalf. The lesson is, she discovered the problem of food supply and took the right action by approaching the first project manager for permission in order to give the solution. According to her, all she needed to do was to give the project managers free samples to strengthen her relationship with them which was seen as the necessary sacrifice to block the link of any potential rival. Another lesson is when you provide a solution to a particular problem; people will pay for it because the world is always in need and waiting for a real solution to the problems of mankind. She was able to increase her profits by being consistent in terms of knowing what was required by her customers in terms of time and quality.

One thing I learned from my mother, she never compromised her standards, come what may. Using communication as a tool to influence and connect with others is another lesson I learned from the other successful people. Success is a reflection of your decisions, attitude, and thinking what could be learned from others either far or near. In learning about successful people over the years, I discovered all or most of them think outside the box which is

THE MYSTERIES OF EXCELLENCE

an essential tool for creating an environment of leadership and greatness from within. Successful people such as Lord Sugar are well known for finding creative solutions using creativity tools such as brainstorming, Imagineering, and other challenging models. A business coach once told me that what he learned from Tony Robbins, the American motivational speaker, enabled him to know and understand how to realize the drivers for strategic change within an organization through effective communication and how strategic thinking could be developed to influence strategies and processes within an organisation which had earned him more clients and business. The coach was able to make miles by earning six times more because he learned from the best in the field of business coaching. In reading books authored by successful people over the years, I realized that being successful had nothing to do with previous experiences and backgrounds. Rather, it is a matter of discovering who you are and understanding your vision. Once you understand your vision you need the determination to stand out from the crowd by developing a reasonable strategy to create significant value in meeting customer's and client's needs. Another element to be considered in being successful is the tendency of growth, meaning that profitability and productivity need to be included in strategic planning because without growth success can never last.

Attending seminars is another way to meet and learn from the best. Attending seminars I got to know and understand more about converting strategic initiatives to reality and the key factors responsible. Nick Vujicic, was a source of inspiration to the lives of many. In one of his DVD's, *"No arm, no arm, no worries"*, he stresses the importance of believing in oneself by suppressing negative thoughts that only limit you and has you visualizing negativity rather than positive reinforcement. He said, he once believed he would never be able to get married, get a better job or have a life. The only reason most people find themselves limited and not able to go far in life is because they weren't ready for anything. What is around them determines their faith, actions, and thinking. They are fond of saying they could do this only if that had happened, *"I could have gone far only if my father had a white house or black horse"*, the slogan of a lazy man. Nick Vujicic said to make it in life all that needs to be done is to concentrate on what you want to do and be comfortable with who you are and what you have, what a powerful lesson. He shared his experience of how people see and look at him and wonder why he smiles. Their beliefs were a result of his 'no limbs' situation and considered him to belong to a specific class, but he believes he can make it by applying the right principles. As a matter of fact, never believe or accept that you are not good enough or you are not worth anything. The fact is, I would never blame anyone telling you trash that needs to be deleted. Rather, I would blame you for believing the trash, because the person telling you that you are worth nothing is either a good for nothing friend, a family member who never lived a fulfilled life and wished you down simply because of a temporary situation or wanted you to settle for less by discouraging you from attaining the next level. No matter the state of a man's life, storms do occur unexpectedly and leads to questions of one's understanding about life, if the storm would ever be a thing of the past and why me or why this time? However, learning good and courageous lessons from the experienced ones could always help you in overcoming such situations. Storms are not good reasons to give up in any good mission by allowing your vision to flee off because, says Ecclesiastes 7:8, *"better is the end of a thing than the beginning thereof"*. Having learned from others for the benefit of yourself, steps need to be taken with confidence and not fear, for both can never dwell in the same avenue. A lot of people are frustrated and angry with themselves and others simply because of their situations. They are afraid to make moves towards making it happen, they've got reasonable excuses and they believe they're worth nothing or they consider it their destiny simply because of the number of wasted years in a direction or path that wasn't theirs. The fact is, such people would continue being in their unpleasant situation until they begin to learn the right principles from the right people in order to become successful. Mike Murdock who is the host of "The Wisdom Keys", a television show, said he usually designs the cover of each book he writes before writing because that keeps him on course while writing, meaning that having a picture of your time goal in terms of what you want to be and where you want to be would enable you to embrace the right pattern towards successful moments.

Most people do get stuck at one point or the other and as a result, they're jump-starting, which means they are not waiting for the right time before moving. They follow another person's success and try that path but fail because that wasn't the right venue for them. Moving in any direction without proper investigation and understanding succeeding parameters being in line with your passion and ability is the first step towards failure. The ability to discover and understand is what creates uniqueness in anyone, mostly when moving in a particular direction while remaining evergreen. Many are talented and passionate in terms of music but end up failing after forcing and pressuring themselves to wax one or two albums. These people usually have just jumped into music and never spent the time to discover an understanding of those hidden successful parameters and progressive steps. Studying these steps could enable them to develop a unique pattern in terms of singing, dancing, and staging them, thus helping them go further within the entertainment industry such as Michael Jackson, Lionel Richie and Whitney Houston. Their big mistake is that they spent time and other resources trying to emulate superstars rather than taking insights from the so-called superstars. They become copycats, the fact is I have yet to see photocopied documents, either colored or black and white, having more authenticity than the original. In most cases, people who imitate others aren't aware of the limitation and negativity they are exposed to, the faith and confidence to face down challenges in order to go miles in a courageous manner would always be lacking. Once a man can't go further in any direction, the hard and gospel truth is such a man would eventually run on another man's track and also have his life lived by another man. Many do consider themselves ignorant for not seeking and listening to the right and applicable advice. Instead, they chose to apply the wrong strategy in which they ended up and landed them in an unexpected position at an unexpected time. Most people fail in their endeavor not because they have a bad intention but because they ignore the gradual process of learning that the major platform in understanding the basic requirements will attain movement in a specific direction. The fact is the more one could be comfortable in ignoring the realistic and applicable principles regarding a particular direction while embracing sentiment due to its convenience in terms of time, quality and cost, the higher the tendency of failing in the long run.

    Many people do not understand the mysteries of progression that would enable them to identify and understand the next step before the conclusion of one step. King Solomon said in the book of Proverbs: *"Prepare thy work without, and make it fit for thyself in the field, andafterward build thine house"*. This passage reflects the role of effective strategic planning before execution. Many

THE MYSTERIES OF EXCELLENCE

people execute without having an insight of what the next step is going to be and that makes them stagnant at one point or the other. Many start their building without having the full capability of finishing it due to lack of real preparation. The fact is, to be prosperous in an endeavor; you must start from developing your passion or talent by investing in what it requires, such as time and other valuable resources to make periodical and expected growth towards attaining excellence. Many live a half-fulfilled life simply because they preferred quantity rather than quality in all they accomplished. Bear in mind, attaining and living a quantity life is easier and cheaper but never stands to survive the test of time, reality, and value, they might be content but where there is still room for improvement more could still be done. Living a quality life requires making a huge sacrifice in terms of time and money it's only for those who are intellectually fit and equal to the task in terms of making strategic decisions based on the content and not the container of a particular item. However, some of the paramount lessons are to learn from the best to become profitable and relevant is the ability to read between the lines and understand every blue or smaller print before getting committed to a term or condition. Many people have lost lifetime fortunes, even court cases because they signed without reading or understanding the terms and conditions attached to a sale or lease of a particular business or property and later end up being trapped. The best are well known for employing the service of an expert in most of their transactions and they never judge a book by its cover because the image on the cover page of a book might have a particular meaning in which might not be understood by all.

GATHERING THE REQUIRED INTELLIGENCE

"Intelligence without ambition is a bird without wings".

-Salvador Dali

Both professors Resing and Drenth describe intelligence as: "The whole of cognitive or intellectual abilities required to obtain knowledge, and to use that knowledge in a good way to solve problems that have a well-described goal and structure." From this definition, intelligence requires *intellectual abilities*, meaning the capacity to make use of our senses to take in, compare, and recall data for specific judgments or decisions regarding a situation. In a nutshell, intellectual ability refers to the skills required to think critically, see the connections between disciplines and the problem solved for a new or changing situations. Intellectual abilities create the right platform for critical thinking. *"To obtain knowledge"* is another fact mentioned in their definition, as a matter of the serious quest for intellectual growth and self-improvement, the need to obtain knowledge has been on the rise over the years. Knowledge can be obtained through constant practicing, having a desired goal in mind. It could be obtained by asking the fundamental questions such as "When?", "Where?", "How?", "What?", and

"Why?" and also through experimenting with new ideas or methods. Observing the occurrences and outcomes of various situations and listening to others is a very good platform for learning and also vital in our everyday life in relating with others. Reasoning with others in a logical way is another way of obtaining knowledge. The major reason for gathering intelligence in any endeavor is to solve problems and achieve desired goals through specific planning and strategies. Intelligence becomes relevant and irrelevant within seconds, mostly when embarking on long-term projects. Therefore, an excellent mind needs to be updated in terms of intelligence; it is required to be successful and to be regarded as an achiever in any endeavor. A three-year public project was awarded to a project manager who forgot to consider the inflation rate before bidding for it. He later asked for more funds to complete the project in which the local authorities invited for scrutinizing, it was later realized he mistakenly underestimated the project cost and he was regarded as being incompetent. It was assumed he didn't know and didn't have what is required to complete a project successfully, which made him ashamed of himself. However, in gathering intelligence, it is paramount to know the impact of what could be required at various points of a project. This reflects an understanding of the situation and the potential appropriate action which needs to be taken mostly in preventing unexpected situations, such as financial losses or any form of damage to a personal or organizational reputation.

In today's world, the two types of intelligence needed in order to remain at the top of your game are emotional intelligence, which enables you to study and control your emotions as well as the others. This ability is a necessary requirement in building relationships and to display appropriate feelings. The second most important form of intelligence is social intelligence, and it involves

GATHERING THE REQUIRED INTELLIGENCE

understanding social situations, relationships, and knowing what to do in any given situation. Understanding others and when to gather intelligence is another parameter for attaining excellence in any endeavor because it indicates the impact of time in implementing strategies. Forecasting budgets effectively and utilizing resources can never be possible without the gathering of the right intelligence. Another parameter to be considered is where the gathered intelligence is required, what it has to do with each location and at which particular events takes place. Giving intelligence at the wrong time, place, and quality makes the intelligence irrelevant for your purpose.

No matter the activity or role being executed and regardless of anyone talent, there is still a huge need for intelligence. According to Veronica Pamoukaghlian, in one of her articles: *"The result is that individuals who may have the talents to succeed in life may be labeled as unintelligent, whereas some of those labeled as intelligent may be less endowed with such talents"*. However, the only thing that gives the ability to adapt to the environment and to learn from experience in becoming successful is intelligence. It enables you to achieve your goals in life. Intelligence enables you to capitalize on strengths while improving on your weaknesses and also improves your practical abilities. In reality, intelligence needs to be well analyzed and well utilized to get the best of it, else it would be a waste of time and resources. Another importance of gathering intelligence before execution enables you to position yourself at the right place, the right time and for the right purpose. This might require one to change their thinking, behaviors, and knowledge patterns to avoid wastages. In business, it enables you to study and analyze market conditions to make the right predictions and draft effective strategic planning for future trends and demographic targets.

THE MYSTERIES OF EXCELLENCE

    A few years ago, I got to realize some peoples' lives had been lived by others simply because they failed to discover their true passion and right direction and also failed to gather the required intelligence in getting to the top of the mountain they desired. Such people refuse to understand that regret needs to be eliminated before it appears by taking the right steps with the accurate information to make right decisions regardless of how a situation might be. Many blame their family's background for their failure after spending part of their life not discovering their direction which is as a result of not gathering the right intelligence at the right time to make the right decision. Some wasted their life doing what wasn't theirs as a matter of greed and some out of confusion by family members, friends, and colleagues, yet it is your major responsibility to discover who you are, what you want to be, what is required of you to become whatever want to be. Discovering the people and things in your life that help by inspiring you to face down the unbelievable and unexpected challenge is of the utmost importance. Another fact I came to realize is that most people wishing to excel in life never grow and develop intellectually because of their traditional ways of doing things. This leads to achieving the same result like that of their great grandparents, they are well known for kicking against new ideas or reluctant to adapt to change at the right time. Procrastination is another force that disallows many from doing whatever needs to be done at the right time for success to be accomplished. Further research revealed procrastination as the act of doing more pleasurable things in place of less pleasurable ones or carrying out less urgent tasks instead of more urgent ones, thus putting off impending tasks to a later time. I wonder how and when those dwelling in the town of procrastination would get to the top because it's the deepest valley ever seen or known.

    A gospel minister going to preach without being prepared

GATHERING THE REQUIRED INTELLIGENCE

on what to talk about might end up spending hours without a clear message. Gathering intelligence prepares you for future challenges, to avoid doing things anyhow, and lost opportunities. According to Alice Waters:

> "This is the power of gathering: it inspires us, delightfully, to be more hopeful, more joyful, and more thoughtful: in a word, more alive".

The act of gathering intelligence reflects on what you are going to do and how to go about it. Gathering intelligence enables you to build a strong relationship with the right and required stakeholders to enable you to accomplish your goals in life, in which I would like to suggest you read *"The Seven Principles of Transformation"* written by Emmanuel Goshen. Learning how to create and use networking platforms such as a generation of referrals to Increase business and opportunities are advantages of gathering intelligence. Getting the right connections and advice from others to increase your confidence and raise your profile with the aim of being a positive influence on others is always a result of gathering intelligence. Many people have been unable to live up to expectations and are hopeless in advancing their life simply because they lack the right intelligence. Robert Kiyosaki discussed the fact that many people are being misinformed by the media, school and home in his book '*Rich dad, Poor dad.*' The fact a man who knows how to think in the right manner and is fulfilled would never forget to train his children to do likewise. The right intelligence enables you to be whatever you want to be, needs to be searched for and not waited for. The ability to gather intelligence creates the platform to discover the genuine wisdom of applying the right knowledge provided you've understood your calling and passion which are the major components needed to excel

THE MYSTERIES OF EXCELLENCE

without any form of doubt. King David wrote in Psalm 90:12, *"Teach us to number our days, that we may gain a heart of wisdom"*, which means that having the right insight of what to do at the right time is expected of us, likewise growth is expected of us as the number of our days increases. Wisdom is the principal key for anyone to excel, which is a result of gathering the intelligence from reasonable and reliable sources such as coaching, training, networking and other forms of learning. However, intelligence needs to have a reasonable necessity attached to it to make this particular intelligence valuable.

EMBRACING PROFESSIONALISM

"Just as your car runs more smoothly and requires less energy to go faster and farther when the wheels are in perfect alignment, you perform better when your thoughts, feelings, emotions, goals, and values are in balance".

-Brian Tracy

First and foremost, knowing what professionalism is and embracing it are two different things. Professionals are known for their specialized knowledge and also understand every corner of their respective fields. They've made a deep personal commitment to developing and improve their skills, and where appropriate, they have the required training, degrees, and certifications that serve as the foundation of various kinds of knowledge to solve and handle complex issues and situations.

Investing in any aspiration without recognizing the role of professionalism is like a ship without a destination. However, professionalism is not just dressing nice or having an advanced degree. According to dictionary.com, the definition of professional includes the following:

> "expert in the field which one is practicing, excellent practical and literary skills in relation to the profession, high quality in work, high standard of

ethics, reasonable work morale and motivation, appropriate treatment of relationships with colleagues, and commitment to the field".

Professionalism is important to both leaders and their organization as a whole because it is a platform for leading with the expected standards aiming at higher success by creating better relationships with stakeholders. Professionalism reflects the development and intellectual ability to handle complex issues in any given situation. A leader or an organization known for professionalism would be respected for their level of competence, conduct, approach, and qualities. It goes along with understanding the technical or ethical standards to operate at the highest level in any field. Take note, being a professional wrestler and being a professional boxer are similar in a few situations because they are both sports that involve more than one and both contenders need to contend for a reason. On the field of play, though, the games have different rules. Wrestling is more beating your contender till he gives up at the count of three, whereas boxing is about the throwing of punches at your contender that needs to carry weight to either accumulate points for yourself or knock your contender out of the ring, each punch thrown should never be aimless but for a specific reason. This is what makes you a professional and the punches also need to do in a technical way. But the point is a talented boxer without a professional trainer would never be able to go miles career-wise because knowledge of keeping one's weight balanced on both feet, keeping one's feet apart as to move and maintain good balance is part of your training. One thing I noticed is that boxers make moves studying their contender's potential action and are always on the alert either to throw punches or to hide that of the contender. It requires the impact and service of a professional trainer for a boxer to understand the four main types of punches (Jab, which is a sudden punch; Cross, which is a straight punch; Hook, which is a short side punch; Uppercut, which is a short swinging upward punch) and which situation to apply them and not just doing things any which way in the ring. However, in wrestling, kicking your contender as many times as possible is allowed but in boxing, it is against the rules and could lead to disqualification in most cases. The fact is, without the act of embracing professionalism I doubt if any leader or organization could excel in a competitive environment. Likewise, public figures and celebrities need to be professional when they are in public because people see them differently and their words and actions make headlines.

Likewise, to excel in any field, professionalism can't be ignored by sticking to sentiments and not facing the reality in terms of what it requires attaining excellence. The fact is professionalism encompasses a number of different attributes in terms of its definition as *"the conduct, aims, or qualities that characterize a profession"*. The attributes of professionalism create a pattern to reflect the specialized knowledge needed to succeed in any field. An individual or organization is serious about doing the hard work which makes an individual relevant and keeps updated with any form of change taking place within the profession to ensure the regular delivery of exceptional service. For an organization's reputation to stand out within any industry, the role of professionalism can't be ignored or underestimated. However, the attributes of professionalism includes:

APPEARANCE

The English romantic fiction novelist, Jane Austen once said:

"Nothing is more deceitful than the appearance of

humility. It is often only carelessness of opinion, and sometimes an indirect boast".

As commonly said in the business world, looking good is doing business because it attracts potential clients who need someone who is capable of helping them solve their problems. Beatrice Ledbetter was made an investment manager just six months into her training simply because her appearance attracted an unknown entrepreneur whom she convinced to invest millions of dollars into her company. Another fact is, appearance reflects the manner in most cases because people take you for real or granted based on your appearance; the impression they perceive about you might maintain a business relationship for a long period of time. Appearance is one element of professionalism and creates an avenue to be welcomed and received with maximum respect in any gathering. I have seen a lot of people whose communication skills are below the expected average and treated with integrity due to their appearance. Businessmen are usually expected to dress in business casual attire or suits and ties. Dresses, pantsuits or suits are appropriate for businesswomen. Any field you may find yourself in, you must also clip your nails, get your hair cut regularly and show up for work or business cleanly shaven or at least keep your beard neatly trimmed. Appearance helps organizations project the right image with clients and the public. Appearance boosts your confidence mostly when addressing or presenting a business initiative to an audience of business and corporate leaders.

COMPETENCY

"No human being will work hard at anything unless they believe that they are working for competence".

-William Glasser

Professionalism is not just getting things done for the sake of it but with the required insight and competence which helps in laying your foundation towards distinction. It is not necessary for a leader to become a jack of all trades by trying to perform or know all functions required to move an organization forward or to remain unchallengeable within a specific industry. Employing other professionals to get the job done also clarifies what the company's expectations are of their leaders. Making them reliable and accountable for their actions, provided they've gotten the freehand to operate and make decisions within a specified limit and expectation, will keep a company's reputation solid and professional. Professionals don't believe in reasonable or tangible excuses but focus on finding solutions. They strive to become experts in their field, which sets them apart from the rest of the pack. This can mean continuing your education by taking courses, attending seminars and attaining any related professional designations. The act of competence in professionalism facilitates effectiveness in anything worth doing. Many authors do claim professionalism as an end product of educational background and experience, but without competence, attaining excellence remains impossible. Competence also entails a certain degree of autonomy and self-direction. In other words, you know what needs to be done without close supervision, and it requires you to be organized and keep track of completed and uncompleted tasks. In order for you to understand and respect the context of competency, you need to know and understand what is expected of you at any given time, the best decision to be made and the accurate time to make such decisions. However, the professionalism in any individual would always enable them to think differently in complex situations. Competency is what is required to hire the right people for the right position which always enhances success for an organization. Having the right competencies empowers your team with the right knowledge (the facts and information required to expand one's experience), values (the required and expected ideas to be shared by the members of an organisation about what is good for the progress and common interest of all), behaviours (the expected pattern of way of controlling one's acts or conducting oneself, especially towards others within an organisation), abilities (the proficiency in a particular area to perform and deliver to expectation) and skills (the vital requirement to become an expertise). Competency drives affordability and accessibility and it's very vital in reviewing and evaluating the performance of team members.

HONESTY

A dishonest man is the one without value and can never be regarded or singled out for excellence. Honesty is the act of telling the truth in facts and figures which creates the platform to be trusted and not likely to steal, cheat, or lie. Honesty goes along with truthfulness and integrity. An organization well known for honesty would always reap the dividends of a good reputation because, without it, leadership is meaningless. *Leadership depends very much on reputation to relate and operate in the outer world in what took a long time to build but five minutes to ruin,* according to Warren Buffett, the American business magnate. The fact is it takes honesty to build, maintain, and sustain a reputation. Honesty is a vital behavior pattern for leaders to build in employees, mostly those at the front desk dealing directly with the customers. Warren Buffett's second rule states: Being trustworthy and inspiring trust in those around you. If you commit to doing what you say you'll do, people will come to trust you. By being trustworthy and, therefore, a good role model, you can inspire trust in others. No matter how talented a man may be, without honesty in his actions, words and relationship with others, such would end up being limited at one point or the other. Honesty is fairness and straightforwardness of conduct towards all, meaning relating with all in the same manner and share things equally regardless of the facts or what the situation might be. Honest people never compromise their values when in a position of power or money which reflects their real personality. Another product of honesty is the reflection of maturity and self-acceptance, and it also fosters courage and connection. For anyone to be regarded as honest, one needs to examine his attitude towards others, do I like the shortcut or take the harder road? Am I trustworthy? Do I take responsibility for your mistakes, omissions, and shortcomings? Are my actions predictable and congruent with my stated positions? Do I follow through on my promises and avoid making excuses? Are my behaviors dependable? Lastly, do I cherish my values? Bear in mind, honesty never dies or grows old but would always remain helpful. Honesty enables you to demonstrate confidence fearlessly. When you are honest, you are forthright about who you are and what you do and will accomplish your goals.

THE MYSTERIES OF EXCELLENCE

INTEGRITY

The late musical legend, Bob Marley once said:

> The greatness of a man is not in how much wealth he acquires, but in his integrity and his ability to affect those around him positively.

Integrity is a vital part of leadership and professionalism, without it, hardly anyone can create a positive influence on others. Integrity is about facing the reality of a particular situation and not taking shortcuts for the sake of anything, it gives the full confidence to stand your ground regarding the actions you take and decisions you make both in life and at work. It enables others to see and take your vision and strategies as authentic. A man with integrity is the man with moral principles and commands respect without struggling for it. Integrity goes along with the attitude of reflecting honey and accountability mostly when in a position of trust within an organization or public office. A man with integrity would ensure he is genuine and consistent in his relationship with others around him who makes it easier for others to trust and take him for his words and personality. It requires integrity and competency before anyone can be assigned to a high-level responsibility. The American television personality, Oprah Winfrey, said: real integrity is doing the right thing, knowing that nobody's going to know whether you did it or not. In the context of reality, integrity is not pretending to be something you are not, by speaking or walking in a different form due to the presence of some friends or dignities, the unchangeable fact is pretenders are always long-term failures simply because they are putting on another's man's shoes. Integrity would always earn you respect and yet it requires you to be yourself and remain professional. What the highest currency leaders trade on is trust. If there is trust between leaders and those they lead, any reasonable goal is attainable. Without trust, even the simplest objective is a hill too high to climb. In a nutshell, it takes integrity and courage to carry others along, and also to excel in any endeavor. Leaders or organizations who stand and relate with integrity would always face huge challenges in attaining a leadership position in any industry but the tougher the tide and waves, the more interesting their story becomes. Another fact on integrity I learned is that wealth can come and go, but integrity will always remain forever because it is reaping the credibility of whatever others know of you. Integrity as one the parameters for excellence could be developed by keeping to one's word, establishing reasonable and consistent principles as a code of conduct to guide an organization's activities and also uphold its reputation. However, to be seen as a man of integrity, fairness and equality need to be your watchwords. To sum it up, at this point lack of Integrity can make one worthless in public sight and make one unfit for greater opportunities and responsibilities. It can also destroy any business because public members are top stakeholders to any business, they've got a powerful voice and that can't be underestimated.

ACCOUNTABILITY

Professionalism also includes holding yourself accountable for your words and actions, especially when you have made a mistake. Accountability is about taking the reward and in turn, the reward for the action of others. It tells more of your impact on an organization either positively or negatively. Businessdictionary.com defines accountability as the obligation of an individual or organization to account for its activities, accept responsibility for them, and to disclose the results in a transparent manner. However, without accountability, no value can be attached to any activity of any leader. In embracing professionalism, how accountability is demonstrated within an organization essentially defines the working relationships fundamental to every activity that occurs within it. Accountability needs to serve as the guiding principle that defines how leaders and other stakeholders make commitments toward each other, how progress is being measured and reported, how situations are being handled, mostly when the unexpected happens and how much ownership needs to be taken. The real power of accountability lays in the ability to effectively and clearly define the expected results you would be holding others responsible for, provided all resources required are made available. All training efforts and improvement processes need to be made with a clear focus on any results you want to achieve both in life and at work. However, all efforts need to be imbued with expectations of progress at various levels as to guarantee overall success.

    Attaining excellence, significance or being a good leader is never easy or simple, but the only way is by practicing professionalism regardless of what you do or the height you are standing. It is about maintaining a high standard in terms of behavior, appearance, productivity and workplace ethics. It is a platform of helping stakeholders gain the confidence to deal with change, improve their working relationships with colleagues and take more accountability for the impact of their own behavior on the working culture of the organization. Professionalism needs to be the foundation for effectiveness in leadership, customer service and satisfaction, and investment. Professionalism is also about following exceptional guiding principles to the letter and not giving excuses. Nothing else is required in minimizing conflict within an organization or in a negotiation environment other than professionalism. It reflects what the values and expectations of an organization or a political party stand for. On the other hand lack of professionalism would reduce the level of motivation and commitment among employees by not giving their best at various stages which result in lower productivity. Things are done in an irresponsible and unethical manner where professionalism is lacking.

MANAGING RESOURCES EFFECTIVELY

"Success in management requires learning as fast as the world is changing."

-Warren Bennis

In laying the foundations for success, it is paramount to have an effective management in place, it helps relationships, project and customer managers to define and understand the scope of their responsibilities and challenges them in delivering excellence other than a common service which places on the same line with your competitor. Bear in mind, for resources to be well utilized, your management system needs to be effective, nothing more or less. As a leader, you should be able to know and forecast what your strengths and weaknesses are which would give you a reflection of what you are capable of doing both currently and in the future. In managing and utilizing resources leaders need to ensure that their managers understand what strategic plans are and how best to implement them, and when it is best to change or review a particular strategy in relationship to the variances of external factors. As I do tell my clients, being successful in business, career, ministry, and life is always a result of getting the requirements right and nothing more. In reality, those

MANAGING RESOURCES EFFECTIVELY

managing your resources need to be experts who are capable and passionate of separating high risk issues from those which are side issues, capable of developing and getting more business, clients and customers and not those who have nothing to offer, only interested in consuming the allocated hours and always awaiting payday which is not the best of it all.

For a better understanding, organizational resources are so vital to any business regardless of their size, it has a lot in determining the life and extent of an organization. There is the required input for leaders to capitalize on how to show their worth, no leader can get things without the required resources. In a nutshell, resources need to be valued because those are the assets that a corporation would always and can always depend on for production processes. There are five basic types of organizational resources: human resources, financial resources, monetary resources, raw materials, and time. One resource would have to depend on another to produce results such as quality and effectiveness.

The role of effective management is to enable leaders to design the required framework to manage an organization's policies, procedures, and processes in utilizing its resources and enable it to promote continual improvement within. Having an effective management system enables organizations to increase their level of profitability by equipping its managers to understand and apply best practices in approaching both common and uncommon workplace situations and handle them effectively with the aim of increasing earnings and decreasing cost and liability within an organization as a whole. Effective management also includes training managers in the aspect of sales growth along with how it could be measured and managed. In increasing the level of profitability, it is paramount for leaders to cut out unprofitable products and services, target new customers from within groups, also focus on the valuable ones, and focusing the right demographics by studying variance at different time and situations. Also researching new technologies is a way of getting things done easier and faster. However, increasing profitability isn't rocket science. It just requires a logical approach and incorporating the right strategies, by consistently creating and giving customers what they want, an organization can maximize profit margins in the short term and ensure they remain competitive in the future.

The need to improve productivity is another benefit of having an effective management system because it entails the efficiency with which a firm convert inputs into outputs in ensuring an organization's goals are met with limited resources which needs to be tightly managed. The importance of effective management goes a long way in aiding organizational processes which include strategic planning, setting goals and objectives, managing and utilizing of resources, deploying the required human and financial assets to achieve objectives, and measuring results. It also includes recording and storing facts and information for later use or for others within the organization. Management functions are not limited to managers and supervisors but every member of the organization has some management and reporting functions as part of their jobs such as time and objective. No ifs, and's, or buts, effective management invariably results in business success, all things being equal while ineffective management often results in business failure.

Effective management is the key to high performance within an organization, provided stakeholders understand the vision of an organization. Effective management makes way for the applicable skills and strategies in achieving expected goals within an organization. Likewise, in managing effectively, the role of effective communication can't be ignored or underestimated because, without it, there are bound to be conflicts and confusion because it becomes impossible to coordinate activities within an organization for the purpose of attaining excellence. Employing effective management models enables leaders, managers, and all stakeholders to act fairly and consistently towards using a broad range of strategies, systems, and processes to manage and lead by providing a clear direction and guidance for setting clear goals and objectives. In attaining, excellence leaders need to value people, believe in the effectiveness of teamwork, be able to demonstrate leadership with a clear direction and hold managers accountable and responsible without punitive measures. Prioritizing customer needs to be at the center of strategic plans and implementation, creating talent management strategies to develop essential skills in various individuals such as communication, people management, and other vital aspects. There is always a need to plan effectively by considering all reasonable parameters before execution to avoid wastages. As a leader, you need to ensure that before employees are promoted to management positions or placed in a position of trust, the ability to manage needs to be tested and confirmed because it has a lot to do with the reputation of an organization.

   Stability is another benefit of employing an effective management because it enables leaders to carry others along with compassion by being reasonable and realistic in their relationship. Being stable enables anyone to identify and understand the time and core parameter before acting towards success. When a leader is stable, his team members would eventually know what to expect and what is expected of them. They would work with confidence in a consistent manner and in a clear direction manner once the big picture is made known and understood. Once stability is being injected into any management system, attaining excellence would never be problematic because stakeholders would always feel more relaxed and confident about their future, any form of change or new initiatives would be seen as sensible and not as a threat to stability would always serve as a guide through the process. The need for stability cannot be ignored because if leaders become unstable under various forms of pressures, such events would see them as struggling or just feeling overwhelmed with their roles and this may lead to becoming vulnerable. In order to afford not becoming unstable, leaders need to be honest and courageous in sharing their vision while leading others and checking out for bottlenecks and potential risks before they occur. Excellence is attained by a gradual process in which every process requires taking steps at every expected period. However, when an athlete moves before the gun shot, the athlete gets disqualified because he moved before the expected period and the opportunity for said athlete to show what he can do would also be wasted. The need for opportunities to be created within any organization is to make leadership and management effective, it has enabled leaders and managers to understand the need to inspire, empower and facilitate excellent performance to operate at the peak of any industry. To clear the air, interacting with others creates the opportunity for leaders to view and consider the thoughts and expectations of others, also knowing when and where to support and develop newly discovered talent which is vital for success. Leaders who believe in creating opportunities for others to discover and grow are well known for championing a positive approach and impact towards change and delivering positive outcomes. Many leaders believe in leading with a high level of charisma to gain more respect and not showing others how to lead effectively, such have always lost their opportunity to leave behind a lasting legacy. Leading is not imposing on others in an unconvinced state to achieve or attain, it is an opportunity to help and serve others towards attaining excellence by helping to being the best they want to be. However, leaders must be honest in ensuring their team members are passionate about their vision, or else it becomes hard to achieve.

Effective management is important to an organization because it involves planning and goal setting, along with team motivation, as to execute the plans in an inspirational manner and just for the sake of doing things. It creates a direction for an organization and communicates its vision both internally and externally in a clear and understandable manner. Effective management is important because it enables an organization to initiate and influence activities and be proactive rather than reactive in its strategy so that it has full control over its own destiny.

Defining critical team roles and responsibilities is another result of effective management to innovate and facilitate problem-solving and effective decision-making processes which reflect performance excellence. A popular African proverb states a problem identified is half solved, but it also requires knowing and understanding the right solution to solve it. Effective management clears the air for leaders to understand and influence possible factors that could affect performance. In most cases, the situation affecting performance could need some motivational approach to change things around. Delegated effectively this can ensure individual and team targets are met as expected.

In a nutshell, effective management is the link between direction and implementation. A direction is the course action of an organization which reflects how it makes moves or operates within any environment, a direction determines the, how's, what's, where's, and when's while implementation is the process of putting a decision or plan into effect which is commonly known as execution. Implementation deals with the how to, where to, when to and what to. However, translating a specific direction into action requires the implementation of required processes that need to be effectively managed. The role of an effective management system in attaining excellence requires leaders to develop a positive "I can do" approach towards facing challenges with little resources. It is all about communicating clearly and managing relationships confidently, embracing team development and increasing productivity which generates collaboration because a tree would never make a forest. In my opinion, it is about giving and receiving feedback for strategic decision making. Helping others to build on their strengths and eliminate weaknesses or fear is another major output of effective management, identifying the major key elements in building a successful team is another way to inspire others to work together to produce intelligence, creativity, and innovation.

As mentioned earlier on, for resources to be well utilized, your management system needs to be effective, lack of effective management would result in failure of providing a clear direction and managers would be unable to create the required standard and give others clear expectations for what is expected of them. Isaac Newton, the English physicist, and mathematician said:

> "Truth is ever to be found in simplicity, and not in the multiplicity and confusion of things".

The fact is that without an effective management of resources, an organization is nowhere in the journey towards accomplishment. In managing resources and investments, you are to have clear expectations and be systematic by not being too rigid or too flexible. Of course, you are in charge and responsible for giving account of your stewardship to stakeholders but yet, you still to need to listen to others to build trust and confidence which are major parameters for

MANAGING RESOURCES EFFECTIVELY

you to progress because a tree would never make a forest and so likewise, you need others to get things done by managing resources effectively. To achieve your goals, you need to recognize the power of effective management in utilizing your resources because it enables you to identify initiatives that could create value and help you structure your life or organization in delivering excellence. However, any leaders or managers aiming at excellence should never embrace a divide and rule model of leadership and never see some of your team members as heroes while underestimating others because the heroes you taught might be pretenders with a different movie. The challenging aspect of managing recourses is the ability to treat and allocate them as expected mostly when stakes are high, yet an effective and diplomatic communication can enable stakeholders to understand the need to make such decisions. In terms of managing humans, leaders, and managers need to manage both the strong and weak to ensure those falling behind are not being left behind. Bear in mind, your health is more important than your job, you need to manage yourself before your job by having adequate rest and breaks to avoid suffering from depression and high blood pressure that could seize your job from you. Leaders and managers need to relate with their followers with sincerity and equality, not with favoritism which has ruined the careers of many in the past. The fact is, in most cases, those being favored end up being a tear in the flesh of those who favored them while unmerited.

BEING PROGRESSIVE-MINDED

"And now dear brothers and sisters, one final thing. Fix your thoughts on what is true, and honorable, and right, and pure, and lovely, and admirable. Think about things that are excellent and worthy of praise".

-Philippians 4:8

Apart from giving excesses, exhibiting fear and folding of arms, talented and knowledgeable people still fail because taking the right action at the wrong time and place is as good as doing nothing. However, the message is what is right and what is good are two separate things. Having the desire to excel is good but putting in efforts within the wrong approach or context makes the situation non-progressive and meaningless. Going to a reputable college is a good thing but not studying a course that is in line with your passion is a waste of time. You might have improved your vocabulary but the certificate might be meaningless, so why go to college spending time achieving something that would be of no use to you? In most cases, young people go to college just to leave home and equal themselves with their friends. At the same seminar which I referred to earlier on, a young lady narrated how her aunt went to university to study insurance at the advice of her uncle, who was then an insurance broker. She had a nice life and a big house. However, while at her finals at university, her uncle had lost his job and all of his friends as a result of the company where he worked, which went bankrupt. The lady spent over a year looking for a job and had to go learn fashion and modeling in which she has now established herself as an authority. Being progressive-minded is an inspirational matter because it is about having the right thoughts in doing things with the right approach in which would land an excellent result. A progressive-minded person would always find it easy to change others for the better due to their experiences at different stages of life. Let's take some insight from the above passage, *one final thing*. This reflects useful advice being given by a loved one to others for the purpose of their betterment and well-being. It is more of an encouragement for the renewal of their minds setting the right platform for excellence, making it their standard in all their endeavors and not settling for less or accepting life's defeats. As commonly known, success and failure are always theend products of our mindset, that's why we need to be progressive-minded by controlling our thoughts in all we think, do and act which is essential towards attaining excellence. The bible also makes it clear in 3 John 1:2:

> "Dear friend, I pray that you may enjoy good health and that all may go well with you, even as your soul is getting along well".

There it is, specifying how we should live and it can only be achieved while having the right thoughts. It requires having a positive state of mind to always think of doing what is true, honorable, right, pure, lovely and admirable, making sure that with the fullness of time, excellence would always be the result. Having positive thoughts in all you do enables you to enjoy the goodness of life as a whole, finding happiness, real friendship, and joy would never be a problem.

THE MYSTERIES OF EXCELLENCE

While addressing the youth in a particular seminar a few years ago, I did ask the question, why only a few were living their dream life? Some said being rich and wealthy is a game of chance, some said it is a privilege, some said making it in life it is all about being lucky, and others strongly believe a good number of those that end up living their dream life waited for those golden opportunities and went ahead to give names of notable people who went from rags to riches such as Sylvester Stallone and some others. A good number of them strongly believe that living a dream life is always as a result of coming from a wealthily family background. My next question was if given the privilege to make a million dollars in whatever way and not being focused in other ways to be more productive, what is your expected result? One said ending up in a mess, so I asked the young man, why? Because if not having the mind of being productive, the million dollars would be gone in a short while, he replied. From his response, it is clear that whatever good thing or situation a man desires would always require him to have the right determination and make meaningful efforts which are the major elements in facing reality towards achieving their desire. Referring to the words of King Solomon in the , it never takes the wrong approach, wrong mindset or shortcut to stand before kings other than being diligent or genuine in one's work while remaining focused and committed. It is just a matter of time your story would be worth listening to because achievements are desirable by many. Apart from it requiring diligence to excel, a diligent man is always prepared before taking any action he plans before execution and expects gradual progress in all he invests in. A diligent man never fears takinga reasonable risk because with his current state of mind, he knows what he's doing and expecting as a result, meaning assessing risk before taking it but yet it needs to be a positive one.

BEING PROGRESSIVE MINDED

As the bible says in 2 Corinthians 9:6:

"Whoever sows sparingly will also reap sparingly, and whoever sows generously will also reap generously".

In reality, our mindset determines how we approach situations and how we approach situations determines what we get as a result. The need to be progressive-minded also applies to our wheel of life such as family, social life, health, finance, business/career, spiritual, and personal growth. Maintaining all those aspects of life at once is always a challenging task and without being progressive- minded it would be difficult to become all around successful. Analysing it one by one, our families are the most paramount aspect of our lives in which we need to cherish and value, it is an avenue where we need to love, serve, teach and learn from each other. We need a place where to share our joys and our sorrows. The mistake is most people are too busy with their career to think of setting up one and later began to express regret at their later stages in life. I came across a lady many years ago at a seminar. During our conversation, she expressed her frustrations after she lost her job in which she got married to for over ten years. She had a passion for being in control of people and situations to the extent that she had no time for anyone else. The last time someone advised her on settling down in marriage, she replied, "Oh that's not a priority". Cutting the long story short, nothing else keeps your companion better than your family; however, a family is a nation in its own world. The young lady wished she had gotten it at the right time because she later realized the value due to her stage of loneliness and money couldn't buy her happiness. Another key aspect of family is the ability to maintain and sustain it from the unexpected crisis which could force one taking an action which is against one's

THE MYSTERIES OF EXCELLENCE

beliefs. I once read a novel written by a middle-aged and ambitious lecturer who lost his political party nomination for a senatorial seat in which he struggled a lot for. The reason was simply because his brother-in-law wanted his influence in getting a high-earning job in the city but he had gotten the required qualification and this lead to an uncontrollable situation between his in-laws and his wife and he was also brought in the ring. Rather than seeking for an alternative job for his brother-in-law, Mr. Lecturer called him a braggart who had nothing to offer, being unknown to him that his brother-in-law overheard this statement. Making the issue a *tit for tat*, the brother-in-law later went on air with three young ladies who happened to be Mr. Lecturer's former students to expose him of his indecent attitudes which later lead to other ladies to testify on air likewise, and this became the headline on various media. Following the story, it was clear that he had been dishonest with his wife and job because those students claimed they *have to* before passing his course. This soiled his integrity at home because his wife did not stand for it and filed for a divorce, the college where he had lectured for years terminated his appointment for an act of distrust and indiscretion as his behaviour could tarnish the college's reputation and also the party dropped him from the race due to negative reputation. The fact is if he had controlled the situation at home, which is the major value of a man, by being diplomatic, by promising his brother-in-law something else for a later date, no one would have heard of his inappropriate acts and he would have gotten a better chance of winning both the party nomination and election which were vital in achieving his lifetime dream. Coming to the aspect of social life, most people do see the negative side of it, no matter where a man desires to be or attain friends, he still has a role to play, they inform, give ideas, motivate and influence positively. Being in control of your social life requires knowing your friend and the positive impact they make in your life. For you to enjoy the impact of any positive relationship you need to be disciplined, determined and focused regarding how you relate with others outside your family. Another reason we need to socialize with each other is that human beings are social animals, and the tenor of our social life is one of the most important influences on our mental health. Without positive, durable relationships, both our minds and our bodies would always fall apart. However, let's get off negative friendships. If you have friends who discourage you and pull you down, it is better to get rid of them. It might be a harsh decision to make for some, mostly the childhood one's yet distancing yourself is always a good alternative. I remember having negative friends in the past, who were good at painting negative pictures while giving ill advice due to their state and situation. After a while I gave it a thought, rather than wasting time and energy resisting them, I let go of them and I was able to focus my energy and time on progressive-minded people and things that made me happy. In terms of finance we need to spend and invest wisely and also seek more opportunities to expand our horizons. The major need for growth both spiritually and personally, is to enable us to improve and better ourselves, to learn, to explore, and develop our abilities towards doing great.

To hit it home, having a progressivemind is the soul of productivity because it enables anyone to make the best use of any available resources such as time, energy, and finance in making the expected progress in any process. Progressive-minded people never get disappointed when they are let down by others because they are not used to placing too much expectation on others. No matter the level of their strength, they are delighted in carrying on with little faith and courage despite the fact they might suffer setbacks and delays, they still believe in seeking alternative routes where possible or try again. The power of a progressive and positive-minded person can never be defeated by any form of life challenges. Progressive-minded people are always curious about learning more, by asking reasonable questions, finding authentic answers for new and better approaches to doing something. Another interesting fact about progressive-minded people is that they surround themselves with positive people and spend time with them because they learn from their attitudes, beliefs, and success patterns. They get more inspired by greater accomplishments which link to excellence. They always desire to drive for progress and improvements aiming at excellence regardless of the situation, they cherish and stick to their vision by visualizing their desire and remaining focused and persistent towards achieving it. They are also critical thinkers because they study situations and generate relevant ideas to solve uncommon issues. Being progressive-minded makes you self-confident and open-mind which enables you to have a positive attitude or outlook which helps in reaching your full potential by being who you are, seeking for the best of others both currently and for the future. In trying to be progressive, it is vital to really renew one's mind in terms of thinking and approach toward situations mostly about whatever is true, honest, just, pure, lovely, and of good report. It is not trying to do everything and be everything, or even doing it in the quickest way possible. Bear in mind, never be satisfied or content with your current achievements else you would be outdated easily and always try your best in remaining inspired and motivated by things money can't buy and not those which it can. Learn how to carry on regardless of who and what might disappoint you next, make the right decisions at the right time by sticking to relevant and applicable principles. Avoid procrastination because the inability to meet up with backlogs makes you less effective and unable to accomplish urgent goals which are the basic

BEING PROGRESSIVE MINDED

requirements to record regular progress. It's also paramount to live your life as if you would be accountable for it tomorrow; this would help you in being and remaining progressive-minded towards having an excellent life.

STRIVING FOR PEAK RESULTS

"Productivity is never an accident. It is always the result of a commitment to excellence, intelligent planning, and focused effort."

-Paul J. Meyer

You are always a product of your previous mindset, as commonly said by many speakers and authors. Apart from being progressive-minded in all we do, we still need to desire the peak results in all we do. Taking insight from the above quote: *Productivity is never an accident.* Taking a critical view of what productivity is, I would like to refer you to buy and read The Seven Laws of Productivity. The book explains in simple terms what is takes to be productive in one's life and the laws that are applicable and realistic to this end. *Productivity is never an accident*, which means that productivity is an end product of one's commitment in addition to a particular desire for a specific purpose, no matter what the case might be. If one remains consistent, paradise is the limit. The quote tabled the three unchallengeable parameters in attaining the peak in an endeavour:

1   *A commitment to excellence,* by giving the required attention and sacrifice for a specific purpose. The longest journey starts with a single

step but yet it requires a commitment to see the journey as a meaningful one and the sacrifice made worthwhile. The reality behind the term sacrifice goes beyond the literal meaning of foregoing something for another, it is a practical state of one's emotions. It involves taking a genuine and positive risk and bearing a serious pain or giving something of great value. If a man sacrifices going to school for the sake of doing business and after eight years of investing all he has is an expectation of huge returns and the government changes the policy governing the specific business unexpectedly, such a man feels the pain of losing his education and not attaining where he desires to be. No matter the consolation he receives, he would never forget the huge sacrifice he made in relationship to his expectation, would he have to go back to school or what next, this would be on top of his mind for a long time. In a nutshell, all things being equal, if there are no changes in the government policy and the man is and remains committed to attaining the peak in a consistent manner, as a matter of time he would excel.

2 *Intelligent planning.* According to Paul J. Meyer, attaining excellence is not just a matter of planning for the sake of it or adopting another plan or strategy and beginning to operate it without catching or understanding the wisdom and vision behind the plan, which makes it an intelligent one. In desiring to achieve peak results, it is paramount to examine all of the risks and opportunities associated with a particular mission towards achieving expected results, most people

like ignoring the Achilles' heel in things they do and expect huge returns and once the unexpected happens or occurs, it floors them or determines their level for a longtime or the rest of their life. It requires intelligent planning to achieve one's goals once the required resources to make a particular vision a reality are available.

3   *Focused effort*, meaning without a focused effort it's so easy for a man to embark on a journey to nowhere. It enables anyone to centre their interest or activity in whatever they are doing to achieve their desires giving in the required performance. The law of focus is well explained in the seven laws of productivity. The desire for a peak result would enable you to understand your purpose in relationship to the required preparation, performance, and procedure in attaining your desired height in life. However, without understanding the impact of preparation, no one can fulfil a specific purpose because it reflects the state of not being realistic or ready to make an impact on anyone and no one would want to waste time with such people. Performances are usually attached to a specific expectation in terms of time and quality of service. If not attached, things would be done anyhow and all efforts could end up being baseless or meaningless. Performance needs to be given a huge consideration in one's life and career because it is all about the significance and without significance there is no recognition. Once an expected performance is set with clarity, the required procedure becomes meaningful and applicable in which it is left up to the individuals to apply the

procedures in the right manner. Bear in mind, the same procedure could be applied to different situations but time and measures might differ based on the reality being faced at various moments. Another fact is in desiring and achieving peak results, you must know and understand how to strive for excellence. Striving for excellence is a huge task and not just a toy game. It is an important aspect of anything we do, as said by our teachers during my school days, what's worth doing is worth doing it well. It involves trying to put quality and value into everything one does, and this attitude tends to separate the achievers from other participants on the field of play and make them stand before kings. Nothing else makes successful people be what they are other than their ability to make rapid strides in their endeavours. This strive for excellence could be made a reality by the initiative to act on available opportunities either far or near. This strive requires the ability to take responsibility for one's life and action alongside with the right time and set priorities. Another fact about this strive for excellence is about having and displaying a positive attitude in various situations both expected and unexpected, in which is the key to being seen as a problem solver. The strive for excellence enables you to go the extra mile in getting things done, developing innovative ideas, and learning new skills. This strive makes you fearless of failure regardless of the number of times attempted.

In striving for peak results, it is pivotal to understand its need and importance. However, you have to be a big thinker, an opportunist and also a good networker because you can't attain excellence all alone. You need to live your life with a sense of clarity, confidence, purpose, and passion. Some other lessons I learned from great achievers are the ability to determine and understand why they need to succeed and be in full control of their lives, time, and resources. The fact is they never allow anyone to live their lives for them. They separate what is important from what is irrelevant by making the best of each available time and other forms or resources. They learn to stay motivated and boost their self-confidence to make their action in a realistic manner. In striving for peak results, you need to know how and when to take initiative, meaning doing the right thing for the right purpose. The ability to get realistic goals with a vision, mission, and clarity are the basic knowledge tools anyone aiming to be successful needs to possess. In my findings, I discovered that setting goals is one of the major mysteries and fundamental components of long-term success and greatness. In striving for excellence, you need to ensure that your planned goals and strategies are capable of driving your life forward and always ensure you remain committed and focused on your planned goals in order to make it meaningful, or else it will simply end up being a wish. Always ensure your goals are feasible, specific, measurable, and also in your hands, which means to be in full control.

Striving for results will always make you the best you can be and make you energetic towards achieving your highest potentials. It is about effective performance and nothing more. It also facilitates the generation of new ideas, creativity, growth, and continuous research for improvements in one's endeavor.

STRIVING FOR PEAK RESULTS

A young entrepreneur once said:

in all, I do I love to maintain my uniqueness in which yield me results and made what I am.

The fact is, this strive for excellence is the cornerstone of efficiency and effectiveness. Going into any common business without setting a particular uniqueness, such as the genuine brand or platform on which you stand for that also differentiates you from others would make you struggle unnecessarily. Another fact is, in striving for peak performance and results, it is paramount to adopt an entrepreneur initiative because in my findings I discovered that successful people are entrepreneurs and also ambitious, focused, goal-oriented, disciplined, well-organized, and meticulous. They set up streams for passive income, which means that they invest in a business that produces them periodical income such as rental income, royalties or interest on loans. Portfolio incomes are another stream of income which successful people invest in, for example, generating income by selling an investment at a higher price. However, successful people never settle or depend on earned income. Anyone aiming for excellence needs to understand the need to welcome business initiatives to enable them to set priorities and direction for increasing wealth. The act of striving for peak results is the mindset of those who believe in taking responsibilities upon themselves and not those who believe in creating and giving excuses. The idea of attaining a peak result is never for average-minded people rather it's for those who believe in giving it whatever it takes to beat limitations and failure which they might encounter in life.

CREATING A LASTING AND POSITIVE IMPACT

"A creative man is motivated by the desire to achieve, not by the desire to beat others."

-Ayn Rand

A youth pastor once asked us many years ago: *Why would you like to become rich?* A lot of answers were given, but there was a common purpose in our answers: we all wanted to become rich because of our selfish interests. However, a few years later, I discovered the purpose of life is to be a shining light and blessing to our fellow humans and let this light reflect the genuine love and passion we should have for each other, which also makes your lives meaningful and worthwhile. Regardless of your worth, achievements or how privileged you are, the fact is your life has a purpose which needs to be fulfilled and without the help of others, your mission might be impossible. Your story is important to many because it helps others to stick to their life ambitions by remaining focused, committed, and realistic. Your dream counts a lot in the lives of many because it enables you to think, grow, and desire the best and not to be content with less. Your choices and determination inspire more than you think, mostly to the ones you lead. Bear in mind, before creating an impact in the lives of others, there is a huge need to understand oneself, passion, and the situation that requires attention. The authenticity of the impact about to be created is another parameter that needs to be understood. It requires standing out from the crowd with confidence, having identified the leader in anyone and ready to change things for the betterment of mankind. Most talented and knowledgeable people were unable to make an impact in the lives of others because they doubted their ability and refused to carry on their vision while remaining on the right direction. Another fact is, identifying your strengths which include your skills and talents which make you be of significance in creating your impact.

There is no recognition for anyone who has nothing to offer or contribute towards the betterment of his fellow human or community at large. Creating a lasting and positive impact has a lot to do with the act of acknowledging the existence, validity, or legality of something new. People talk of establishing a lasting legacy which is a brilliant idea but I see no way people could establish a legacy without creating a positive impact in the lives of those around them. In terms of identifying the leader in anyone, it is not about the position being held or how many people one is in control of, but improving others through reflecting the uniqueness of one's leadership style, values, character, and traits. My friend who worked in the city was unable to make an impact because he was unfulfilled in doing what he wasn't passionate about. The truth is you can't create a lasting and positive impact without a passion or a conviction. Challenging oneself in solving problems for the sake of others is a better way of making an impact. In general, to make an impact one needs to be proactive and to keep looking for opportunities to progress. There is a huge need to be persistent in taking strategic and positive risks in a reasonable manner while turning situations around for the better. In my findings, some of the core behaviors of people who positively impact the world are the ability to dedicate themselves to what gives their life and others a real meaning and purpose, they share their knowledge with others and also develop them, they serve humanity with their heart. However, they are never dictating, but they believe in influencing others towards change. Bill Gates is a good example of a positive impact towards humanity. He has used his foundation, the Bill and Melinda Gates Foundation, to face down development and health challenges in the most under-developed countries. The foundation has created a huge impact in the lives of many by restoring life and hope. According to Harvey Firestone, *the growth and development of people are the highest calling of leadership.* As a leader, you must have the ability to mentor others by getting them involved in positive activities to expose them to growth and new ideas in a responsive manner and not sitting on the bench and awaiting errors to happen before showing others how effective you are, such as eye service. Many in leadership positions fail in making an impact within their team because they are good at giving orders or directives with a commanding voice and are also known for staying responsibilities but love taking credit for the work effectively done; such people are yet to understand the difference between leaders and rulers.

In creating a lasting and positive impact, you need to be committed towards excellence with a specific direction while applying the required wisdom and not seeking perfection because no human being has ever or would ever be perfect. The mission and message of every positive impact need to be progressive, authentic and of a realistic standard. An African proverb says that the *one who intends to cloth another man should have been well dressed.* In reality, before you can create a positive impact in others and begin to be referred to

CREATING A LASTING AND POSITIVE IMPACT

as a model, you need to have identified your vision and linked to core human values and need of life. You need to ensure that your ideas must be able to stimulate innovation and must be able to inspire the collaboration of like-minded people to support your vision in making it a reality. It is paramount to motivate and align teams towards effective performance and execution to increase the effect of the positive impact you intend to create. In creating positivity in the lives of others it is important to build the right relationship and respecting accountability and effective leadership by relating based on goodwill and not with the use of authority which makes you autocratic. There is a need to relate with others based on enthusiasm or with the use of ultimatums, learn how to give credits for the achievement of others and also pass the blame when an unexpected situation occurs in a reasonable manner. To hit it home, never forget there is always strength in unity and not in a one-man game. However, in making your impact a reality there are three major parameters to be considered for others to see you as an icon or legend i.e. aiming for excellence, planning for excellence and exploring excellence.

In creating a lasting impact, it is paramount for you to see the light, hope, and a fulfilled future in yourself and others because investing in oneself and others without a vision would always result in a meaningless mission. However, enabling others to attain an unlimited excellence needs to be the purpose of creating an impact and such impact needs to be laid on the foundation of wisdom which is the principle thing to acquire before embarking on any mission.

In a nutshell, wisdom is the platform from which a vision is to embark on a mission. It is derived and without it, attaining excellence becomes almost impossible. The confirms that *with wisdom the heavens were made.* In reality, creating a lasting impact requires maintaining and sustaining the vision and life in one's philosophy, which deals with the

THE MYSTERIES OF EXCELLENCE

fundamental nature of reality, existence, knowledge, values, and reason attached to it. Moreover, no matter where you stand or what you want to be, having and applying the right wisdom would serve as a light to guide you through. Considering the impact of light, it is most effective in the dark which gives vision and can also lead to discovery, but there are two major functions of light I discovered its effectiveness and efficiency. The effectiveness of light could be referred to as its ability to produce brightness or vision, meaning the rate at which it would eliminate darkness, while the efficiency could be regarded as the distance visibility could be obtained and the time taken within a specific dark area. The bottom line is anyone aiming at excellence or creating a lasting impact needs to dwell constantly in light; needs to be in the search for wisdom tirelessly and endlessly. Wisdom is not a matter of doing anything for the sake of who is in control. Wisdom is the platform for taking the right initiative which simply means taking the right step at the right time and at the right place. King Solomon said in his book of Proverbs: *Get your outside work done; make preparations in the field; then you can build your house.* In reality, in creating a lasting impact you need to establish your values and vision, get a reasonable strategy in place which includes knowing the cost, time and other forms of sacrifice it might take. The verse could be further explained as having the necessities before thinking for seeking comforts. Most people are unable to complete their houses, meaning accomplishing their goals or visions or missions, simply because they didn't finish their work, which means that by taking effective planning into serious consideration before embarking on their mission, they eventually ended up half way because they weren't fully prepared. Once the foundation of a mansion is noticed to be faulty, it would cost a lot of money in demolishing and reconstructing which makes many people fed up because they

CREATING A LASTING AND POSITIVE IMPACT

see it as a waste of investment. Most people who fall into this circle often discourage others based on their negative experience in what was a result of their ignorance and negligence. In reality, wisdom is the master key to creating a lasting and positive impact in the lives of others. A wise actor would rehearse before performing on stage because if the role is not well played, his reputation might be soiled and might not be called for another role next time he turns up because wisdom is about sticking to and applying relevant and applicable principles in execution and getting expected results.

Aiming for anything in life seems to be easy but attaining it, most especially for the purpose of excellence in all the different aspects of life is never an easy task. There is never a successful journey without serious challenges. According to Brian Tracy, *within you and great success there are great mistakes and failure's,* regardless of your age, experience, knowledge, and race you are never a master of mistakes and it takes years to develop the right habits to achieve this, and the journey is often long and painful. Identifying your values is also a paramount issue to consider before aiming for excellence and creating a lasting impact for others. Identifying your values enables you to make the right choices for your life and what truly matters to you and others. Standing up for a cause reflects your purpose and your uniqueness, it is the true value to fight for and protect. In creating a lasting impact, the major focus needs to be of being of support to others in need and not to exploit others for selfish benefits through dubious means. Connecting with others through effective communication and active listening adds more to your integrity and experiences and enables you to learn about other peoples' needs and values.

In planning for excellence anyone intending to create a lasting impact needs to consider all aspects of the vision from forming the required relationship and the roles of various players i.e. stakeholders. Planning is vital for execution in any situation in which could be the short or long term. Planning has a huge role to play in the process of formulating and implementing decisions about any future direction. Planning is vital for the survival of any vision; else such vision would fade along with time. Planning towards excellence enables you to have an idea of where you want to go, what decisions must be made, and when they must be made in order to get there. Planning has always played a role in matching opportunities and threats with strengths and weaknesses for effective decision making, also setting realistic goals for pursuing a specific mission based on the right and acceptable values and sense of responsibility.

Another fact in planning for excellence is the ability to identify strategic initiative resources, which creates the platform for achieving strategic goals in which includes: Human resources (knowledge, skills, capabilities, and talent); Financial resources (cash, liquid securities and credit facilities); and Intangible resources (patents, goodwill and relationships, etc.). However, physical resources include all the tangible resources owned and used by an organization such as land, manufacturing equipment and office equipment.

Excellence doesn't just happen by magic. It needs to be explored i.e. attaining excellence requires the application relevance principles, because it requires understanding the mysteries in it. In my finding, exploring excellence is about having a quality service for the purpose of growth of all. In terms of quality, the motive is to offer an expected standard for any form of exchange. The term quality represents the value derived for investing resources into a particular organization; quality is a major reputationfor an organization. Service simplifies the unique activity an organization offers to the public in the interest of all.

CREATING A LASTING AND POSITIVE IMPACT

Success could be terminal in some cases, and it needs to be recorded at various stages of a particular project or any endeavor which makes it attain excellence which reflects growth. Success would always be in need of growth to attain excellence, by passing one step before moving to another, the role of growth would tremendously enable fulfillment in terms of enabling the empowerment of oneself with the right knowledge and the required commitment towards making a specific vision a reality and inspire others. However, growth is a necessity for improvements and achieving greater heights also makes any serious- minded person unstoppable. Understanding the principles and need for growth enables us to expand our strength mentally and spiritually. The unchangeable fact is achieving excellence in our work is an integral part of feeling genuinely satisfied in life. This could be learned from successful people and those who impact our lives positively.

Leaving a positive legacy is a wonderful gift anyone could give to mankind but yet it requires one to have excelled in various aspect of life before becoming significant. No one can give what he doesn't have. Not creating a lasting impact for others would eventually make you a disappointment to yourself and others, impacting the words of truth and wisdom to others is the best way to enable them to see the light and make them wise, and not giving money all the while. Authentic leaders are constantly building their legacies by adding deep value to everyone that they deal with by developing them towards the right path, healing the world is the best way to make way to make it a better place for all. Bear in mind, establishing a lasting legacy requires one to be sincere to oneself in terms of knowing and understanding your ability and purpose in relationship to meeting others' needs. However, leadership without impact or significant is meaningless.

TAKE THIS HOME

My sincere message is, there is no opportunity available in the grave, so, therefore, do what you consider being the best of yourself while alive and never look back and never give up regarding your lifetime ambition. Believe in your faith, your ability and what you want to achieve in life. Bear in mind, life owes no one anything and it's your responsibility to strive and get what you want and not waiting for or depending on others because they could only what they have or what they want to give you and not what you want. However, time flies and never waits for anyone which is the major reason to make the best use of it. Taking insight from Matthew 5:14,

> You are the light of the world. A city set on a hill cannot be hidden.

In the context of the passage, the term *light* stands for importance, difference, significance and positive impact to oneself and others. A city on the hill refers to high achievers and not average achievers and for anyone for placed on a hill needs a solid foundation, strong and positive mindset to stand undefeated in any situation either rain or shine. Such a person needs a serious determination, focus efforts, and commitment in terms of stability to stand the test of time and reality. For a city to be built on a hill, the city needs to be unique in all its ways to achieve a better outcome. According to Elbert

TAKE THIS HOME

Hubbard, *'There is no failure except in no longer trying'*. As far you know whatever you are doing or your intentions are, never lose the confidence that inspires you because once the mind is weak, the physical body would hardly win the race. The fact is that failure can be recorded at any point in time unexpectedly and as many times as possible but defeat only occurs when failure is accepted which makes it established. In handling failure in one's journey, it is advisable to break down difficult tasks to make huge challenges easier to overcome alongside with the help of the right ones and as long as one keeps on trying, goals would be eventually achieved, it is just a matter of having the right intention and taking the right approach at the right time.

To make it clear, success is often measured by comparison to others. Excellence, on the other hand, is all about being the best we can be and maximizing our gifts, talents, and abilities to perform at our highest potential. Excellence can only be attained by cultivating the seed of greatness. This goes along with flexibility, patience, willingness to learn, and the use of self-motivation in setting and achieving one's own goals. Excellence starts with the expectation we set within ourselves but a culture of excellence in a team can only be created by the expectation of our leadership. Excellence can be expressed as the quality of being outstanding in any endeavor which goes along with focusing on the need to be done and not procrastinating. Yet, in ensuring excellence, you need to make the right choices without any form of sentiment, personal deceit or pretence because they backfire and make a fool of anyone who's not realistic. Having a better understanding of excellence would enable one to identify it as an attitude and not a skill because attitude reflects your real approach towards situations and would also determine the extent you go, while skills are the special knowledge to back up your approach. In attaining excellence, it is important to cherish and value what you have. While studying the story of Moses in the , a few years ago, he never knew and understood the value of the things he was holding, at least not until he was being challenged by the pharaoh's sorcerers, being faced by the Red Sea, and when the Israelites were in need of something to drink. Bear in mind, what is good is different from what is right as explained in this book but my point is it requires knowing and understanding the right principles to excel in any endeavor and not just the doing what is good. However, doing what is right reflects how sincere and matured one is, in getting things done, also in facing life and its challenges.

    A man with a vision should never be compared to a man with a television. It takes time, money, passion, and endurance for a vision to be made realistic, while a television could be purchased from any store or online, a vision lasts longer than a television. David, the father of King Solomon was appointed by Prophet Samuel and yet it took him twenty years of his life before he was discovered, which was as a result of the challenges of Goliath facing Israel. The stopping block and destiny determinant to the lives of many is what David considered as one of his steps towards greatness due to his previous challenges. However, he was celebrated for making such a bold move. Excellence never occurs by accident but by the determination to break out of limitations which require giving one's best without compromising abilities or standard. Bear in mind, attaining excellence is not just a matter of physical ability but rather the application of intelligence in a consistent manner to solve existing problems. Part of the lesson I learned from King Solomon, despite the fact he was well connected to wealth, power, and fame; was that he never allowed his achievement to dictate or dominate his direction, intentions or values, he was still able to learn from other people and situations around him which made him wiser.

My life aspiration is to impact love, reality, and light to my fellow human beings and never to dominate or exploit anyone for any reason. My vision is to light as many lives as possible and creates positive impacts. A friend of mine once told me, if you light a lamp for someone else, it will also brighten your part. We require patience and perseverance in order to attain excellence because people knowing your intention or passion quickly doesn't mean they would understand it quickly and without understanding it nothing can be done. Keep in mind that the eyes that look are many but those that see are only a few. Joseph, the great dreamer, had the dream of what he is going to attain at the age of seventeen and it took him nineteen years to accomplish it. However, it was never an easy journey, he was about to be killed and to have his dream ruined, and he was thrown into the pit, sold to the merchants only to later become slave. He was tempted ways that could have ruined his dream and then imprisoned for the wrong cause. He was able to excel by the fortune of his gift which made way for him and made him stand before King Pharoah and was to later become Prime Minister; all this from a simple man, to prisoner to Prime Minister. The fact is he had the gift of dreaming and its interpretation before the opportunity of standing before King Pharaoh arose. Another lesson to learn from the life of Joseph is that of endurance, all he experienced before fulfilling his dream was never a bed of roses but the reality is if he had lost his gift or misused it while in prison, I doubt if he would have excelled in anything further.

In my findings, a major attitude that disallows people from attaining excellence is the act of addicting oneself to another man's philology which leads to intellectual dominance and it obscures one from being opened to the right channel of wisdom required to discover himself and follow the right direction to fulfil their dream, make a huge and positive impact also create a lasting legacy. The desire for excellence brings out the institution in one because institutions are built by men with great minds who view and see situations differently from common men. The fact is, a man who can't think for himself is as good as a non-living object because I wonder if a man who can't think before acting would be able to control regular situations not to talk more of overcoming huge challenges and living a purposeful life. Stephen Covey's book, *The 7 Habits of Highly Effective People*, takes a deep insight in Habit 4, which is *Think Win-Win*. Yet, for anyone to think win-win, there is a need for the mind to think independently and not based on a bureaucratic or imposed way of thinking. Unto whom much is given, much is expected, no matter the criticism or discouragement you get from others around you always take the challenge of waxing stronger with your two legs on ground promising never to fail yourself and others around you. Also always stick to well wishes for yourself and others and not showing hatred for others mostly when you lose a game, an opportunity or anything of value at a particular point in time, learn to be courageous and always aim to do better next time because hatred would always metamorphose to pride which goes before a fall.

    I would like to say that having the right insight is an inspirational gift in which is one of the cornerstones in attaining excellence. Insight creates the platform for understanding one's direction also the intelligence for skillful executions. My candid advice, to attain excellence in any endeavour isto never believe in limitations or underestimate yourself, no matter your current situation, how bleak your future might seem to appear, your background or family history, your height, or what the negative ones around think about you or want you to believe about yourself; never give

TAKE THIS HOME

up. As far as leaves and grass remain of the color green, just believe you will make it, provided you are at the right place when you need to be. Remember that underestimating yourself is no more dangerous than poison because it ruins one alive in a creative manner. Avoid negative beliefs, because they only weaken your strong intention and the passion that empowers your soul towards making the required moves. However, your passion is the *light* inside you which guides towards your right direction. The best way to be fulfilled is by living one's life and relating with others with conviction and not confusion, to act with conviction is the ability to do things based on proper understanding while firmly holding to one's belief. My golden points are: learning is the major platform for understanding to occur; understanding your direction is the master key in knowing; applying the right principles towards attaining excellence because it familiarizes you with the do's and dont's in arriving at your expected destination. The next point is, the lack of understanding in any approach makes effective plans meaningless, I do hear many say information leads to transformation but the fact is information does not automatically lead to transformation because information needs to be specific, relevant, required and understandable before it could be utilized in making the necessary changes where applicable and leads to transformation in the long run.

The bottom line is, a man who can't think for himself is as good as a non-living object because I wonder if a man who can't think before acting would be able to control regular situations, talk less of overcoming huge challenges and live a purposeful life. Coming across negative-minded people on a realistic journey aiming at excellence is absolutely inevitable because they are the crabs that found themselves in the bucket and they never want others to go or leave them behind. Rather, they make you lose or waste precious lifetime opportunities by reminding you of previous failures and make use of your current situation to hold you back due to potential disappointments.

I see the issue of being discouraged by others as a normal phenomena of life because many people stop searching for new ideas and find themselves derailed and I wonder why on earth you would allow such people who can't help their situation and improve their standard advise an ambitious person, am sure their advice would end up being Eve's apple which brought down the first man that ever lived according to the . However, it is up to you as a determined and focused person to seek the support of the right people in order to achieve your lifetime ambitions. If you look at the cover page of this book, the picture reflects that attaining, maintaining, and sustaining excellence is never an easy game. It requires the support of others who understand and cherish your vision in a combination of materialistic support and not just well wishes. However, the ability or inability to carry on in light of discouraging situations would always determine how accomplished you would ever be in terms of fulfilling your potentials in life regardless of when, how or wherever you are starting. People would try and frustrate you through various ways mostly when making powerful moves simply because they gave up unexpectedly, so therefore they are minding your business rather than theirs. From my experience as a master coach and inspirational speaker, I got to realize that most of my clients have gotten what it requires attaining the next level but their inability to discover and make use of it kept them stagnant. According to the British novelist, Clive Staples Lewis once said in one of his works during his lifetime, '*You are never too old to set another goal or to dream a new dream*'. This basic concept is applicable no matter what age, race or gender you are. Bear in mind, it is your responsibility to never give up and keep your hopes and

TAKE THIS HOME

dreams alive, mostly when passing through transformational periods because am yet to see a sprinter who opted out either at the starting point or during a completive race and was being celebrated. Note, no one would ever accept the blame for your failures but the same people discouraging you would always like to embrace you once you become significant like in the case of Joseph and his brothers in the .

Sometimes in life, apart from being focused and determined, it becomes necessary to be positively stubborn in order to attain miles in any endeavor. Palm trees are well known for flourishing after passing through a number of stages such as the preparation period, which is about getting the healthiest seed pods from the different exotic palm species and soaked into water for a while, followed by the prenatal period, which is about keeping the seed in a climate-controlled area to encourage maximum growth in a minimal time. However, the seeds are planted in special seed beds with an ultra-rich mixture of humus high-nutrient soil that allows them to sprout more efficiently. The next stage is the infantile period, which is about keeping seedlings in a climate-controlled area where they remain for up to a year. The adolescent period is the next one, during which the seedlings truly start to mature and take on the defining characteristics of young palms such as the distinctly rich green feather-shaped foliage. Once the seedling gets to the mature adult period it can be transferred for plantation, in which its height becomes indeterminable for anyone.

The act of being positively stubborn empowers you with the ability to break through obstructive and unnecessary laws, beliefs, conditions, protocols or clauses which either limit your performance mostly when having a burning desire to go the extra mile in fulfilling a mission, or hinder you from making expected moves at the right time or place. Taking a deep insight from the story of the Israelites in the law of the then Pharaoh, meaning the King of Egypt, at that time gave a serious and controversial condition for the freedom of its people. The law put forth for Moses and the Israelites to abide by was for them to go but not very far. But for Moses to fulfill his mission he needed an "unlimited go" and the "conditioned go." The issue was similar to the man who chooses to give his friend a festival goat and never releases the leash attached to it.

I would like to repeat the fact that the most dangerous situation on earth is being led by a leader without insight mostly when such leader happens to be the rigid type. My question is how would a leader without an insight be able to give accurate direction? The unbeatable truth is the huge price of ignorance would eventually be paid for by the innocent followers. One of the leadership qualities of Moses was, he had an insight of what he wanted before approaching the then Pharaoh and standing his ground to the last point, he was able to achieve his motive because he understands the potential impact of standing his ground.

To draw the curtain, every journey towards excellence starts from the point of taking reasonable steps in order to make one's effort meaningful, it's paramount for anyone who wishes to excel grow with the seed of reality and the insight for greatness and never allow fear and confusion to disallow them from making moves. Once more, anyone who wishes to excel should never be affected emotionally, mostly whenbeing underestimated by others who couldn't help themselves or those trying to take advantage of your current situation. On a final note, the moment you desire greatness and discover your vision, it is your responsibility to understand it by taking the necessary steps. However, the most important thing to be done is to seek no repose till your greatest ambition is achieved, which will enable you to establish a lasting legacy. My father once told me when I was young, "Once a man attains greatness, other benefits would locate him." Attaining greatness is also a matter of being sincere with one's self. The Bible says in Psalm 51:6,

> 'for thou, desires the truth in inwards part and the hidden part thou make me know wisdom'.

In summation, no man gains wisdom and attains greatness without being truthful to himself in all his ways. The gospel truth is, attaining excellence makes one's light shine before others and brings glorious moments and memories to those around them. One powerful fact about light according to the Bible is, it can't be overshadowed by darkness (John 1:5) but it needs to be brought to existence before it could perform its duty and meet its expectation. In reality, before attaining excellence and becoming a shining light, there is a huge need to step out of our comfort zones in order to graduate from the point of challenges to a champion's arena. It takes the continuous desire to succeed in an endeavor before being established as an authority and not one of the issue. Andy Murray, the Scottish professional tennis player never became an authority or recognized as a high profile player in the world of lawn tennis by participating in just a tournament, he participated and won many tournaments such as the Australian Open, the French Open, Wimbledon, the US Open and other international competitions. Attaining excellence has a lot to do with preparation because a student desiring to pass an examination in flying colors wouldn't start reading or studying while the examination commences. Likewise, a farmer hoping for a bountiful harvest would have to take the normal steps of clearing the farmland, sowing and weeding at regular intervals before a bountiful harvest could be recorded at the right time and not by magic because there's time for everything.

www.ingramcontent.com/pod-product-compliance
Lightning Source LLC
Chambersburg PA
CBHW070628300426
44113CB00010B/1696